Beyond Bare Lives:

A Study of a Border Social System in a Southeast Asian Frontier

Sang Kook Lee

Beyond Bare Lives
: A Study of a Border Social System in a Southeast Asian Frontier

Written by Sang Kook Lee

Published and Printed in the Republic of Korea by Yonsei University Press.
50 Yonsei-ro, Seodaemun-gu, Seoul, 03722, Republic of Korea

Tel: 82-2-2123-3378~80
Fax: 82-2-2123-8673
E-mail: ysup@yonsei.ac.kr
http://press.yonsei.ac.kr

ISBN 978-89-6850-715-1 (93300)

₩ 20,000

In memory of Ananda Rajah
(1952-2007)

Contents

Illustrations

Maps

Figures

Photos

Tables

Acknowledgments

This book is an outcome of my long journey spanning almost two decades, starting in the late 1990s. Much of the book derives from my PhD thesis with revisions and addition. I cannot resist looking back on my final days at National University of Singapore (NUS) when I struggled to come to terms with the demise of my great mentor, Ananda Rajah. The book is a long-delayed dedication to him.

While at NUS, many people stood behind me and encouraged me to complete my study. I am deeply grateful to Saroja Dorairajoo for taking over the supervisory role and guiding my study in the remaining period. I thank the other committee members, Carl Grundy-Warr and Kyaw Yin Hlaing for their insightful comments. I also thank Charanpal Singh Bal, Daniel Soon, and Kamaludeen Mohamed Nasir for lending me a hand in writing the thesis. I am grateful to Hing Ai Yun and Eric Thompson for their warm encouragement as then department head and graduate coordinator, respectively.

In Thailand, many people assisted and facilitated my research. I thank Supang Chatavanich and Pornpimon Trichot at the Asian Research Center for Migration, Institute of Asian Studies, Chulalongkorn University for allowing me to be affiliated with the Institute as a visiting fellow. My data collection would never have been possible without help from people in Mae Sot. Above all, I received tremendous assistance from Ekasith in settling down in the field and approaching various groups of people and organizations. I am also indebted to Peter and Supha for their willingness to help me whenever I visited Mae Sot. Friendships with them have made my life in Mae Sot more joyful.

The help the Karen people have given me in my research can never be overemphasized. My research assistant, Plalawla, was most helpful in conducting this research. He assisted me in learning Karen and Burmese and interviewing many Burmese people. A good relationship with the Karen in Mae Sot First Church, including Toe Toe and Paeh, was a source of personal and social well-being throughout my stay in Mae Sot. Besides, I thank many Burmese, though I cannot name them, for their willingness to share their experiences. I am grateful to many NGOs for welcoming me and providing me with research materials.

My gratitude goes to Oh Young Cheol for supporting my research since the beginning of my interest in the Thailand-Burma Borderland in 1999 and Kim Bong Kook for helping me settle in Mae Sot and providing helpful information.

In conducting fieldwork, I received financial support from Asia Research Institute at NUS, Korean Association of Southeast Asian Studies, Sogang University, National Research Foundation of Korea, POSCO Asia Research Grant, and Yonsei University. I appreciate their financial assistance.

An earlier version of Chapter 3 appeared as "Ghettos or Transnational Social Spaces? Burmese Migrant Enclaves in the Thailand-Myanmar Borderland," *Cross-Cultural Studies* 24(1): 99-138 (2018). Chapter 4 is a revised version of "Behind the Scenes:

Smuggling in the Thailand-Myanmar Borderland," *Pacific Affairs* 88(4): 767-790 (2015). In Chapter 5, I draw from "Migrant Schools in the Thailand-Burma Borderland: From the Informal to the Formal," *Asia Pacific Journal of Education* 34(1): 125-138 (2014). Chapter 6 derives from "A Migrant Clinic at the Thailand-Myanmar Border: Legitimacy, Partnerships, and Cross-Border Health Care Mobility," *Southeast Asian Review* 27(4): 77-115 (2017). An earlier version of Chapter 7 appeared as "Borderland Dynamics in Mae Sot, Thailand and the Pursuit of the Bangkok Dream and Resettlement." *Asian and Pacific Migration Journal* 20(1): 79-99 (2011). I thank each publisher for granting permission.

Lastly, I express my heartfelt gratitude to my family. I hope my small effort can pay back my parents' unimaginable sacrifice and love for me. I also thank my brother and sister for their concern and encouragement. Above all, my wife, Kim Sun Hee, has always been with me, going through joyful and sorrowful periods in Singapore, Thailand, and Korea. I hope my work will be a humble appreciation for her immeasurable devotion to me. My son and daughter, Myungjin and Yejin, have become new companions and sources of joy on my journey to the borderland.

List of Abbreviations

ABSDF	All Burma Students' Democratic Front
ADB	Asian Development Bank
BLSO	Burma Labour Solidarity Organization
BMSOH	Boarding Middle School for Orphans and Helpless Youths
BMWEC	Burmese Migrant Workers' Education Committee
BOT	Bank of Thailand
CCSDPT	Coordinating Committee for Services to Displaced Persons in Thailand
CDC	Children's Development Center
CPB	Communist Party of Burma
CPT	Communist Party of Thailand
DKBA	Democratic Karen Buddhist Army
ESAO	Education Service Area Office
GMS	Greater Mekong Subregion
IRC	International Rescue Committee
JRS	Jesuit Refugee Service
KED	Karen Education Department
KNU	Karen National Union
KYLMTC	Karen Youth Leadership and Management Training Center
KYO	Karen Youth Organization
KWO	Karen Women's Organization

LDC	Least Developed Country
MOE	Ministry of Education
MOI	Ministry of Interior
MSH	Mae Sot Hospital
MTC	Mae Tao Clinic
NDF	National Democratic Front
NLD	National League for Democracy
POC	Persons of Concern
SLORC	State Law and Order Restoration Council
SPDC	State Peace and Development Council
UNHCR	United Nations High Commissioner for Refugees
WE/C	World Education/Consortium
ZOA	Zuidoost- Azië

<Map 1> Mainland Southeast Asia

Chapter 1

Introduction

Problem

I grew up with the image of soldiers patrolling along barbed wire fences at the border. Border-crossing risks death, and national news reports have often carried fatal stories on the border of two Koreas. Living a life on the edge is simply impossible. My border-crossing experiences in Southeast Asian borders, particularly the Thailand-Myanmar[1] border, led me to a new world where the border mediates people to build their lives on the move. This book is my attempt to delve into the new world.

The main field of the book is a Thai border town, Mae Sot. Many Burmese[2] stay there without legal status. Although I acknowledge the various precarious aspects of their lives, the normalcy with which they carry on their daily lives has largely been ignored. Although dramatic events often attract our attention, indulgence in cases such as suffering, deportation, drugs, and trafficking does not reveal the totality of the lives of borderlanders at all. Why do they insist on staying there despite alleged hardships? Why is the town not in disarray despite the predominant presence of "illegal aliens"?

---

1 I use "Myanmar" throughout this book instead of "Burma." Since the then military junta had changed the name of the country from "the Union of Burma" to "the Union of Myanmar" on June 18, 1989, the choice of the term among individuals and various groups became a political act even during the so-called "democratization period" from 2010 to February 1, 2021 when the military staged a coup. Those engaging in democratic movements tend to use "Burma," while scholars often use both names interchangeably. My name choice does not necessarily reflect a political stance but is to maintain consistency in naming the country throughout the book.

2 The term referring to "people" in Myanmar has also not seen consensus after the official change in the country's name. Some people refer to them as "Burmese" while others refer to them as "Myanmarese." I use the term "Burmese" when referring to people in Burma; while adopting "Burman" when pointing to the majority ethnic group in the country.

I seek to delve into borderlanders' lives in contrast to earlier works that focused on the borderlanders' problems and victimization. Minghi (1991: 17) points out that there is a tendency for traditional border studies to view "the boundary as an interface between two or more discrete national territories and subject to problems directly reflecting the relations between the nation-states it divides." In the sense that states are desperate to mark "our territory" against "others" (Wilson and Donnan 1998: 9), it is evident that borderlands inherently contain certain levels of conflict between neighboring states and states' aspirations for dominance and independence.

However, borderlands are also living environments where ordinary people root their mundane everyday lives. As Donnan and Wilson mention (1999: 4), borders are "meaning-making and meaning-carrying entities, parts of cultural landscapes which often transcend the physical limits of the state and defy the power of state institutions." Borderlanders, though they lack legal status, make the border town a living environment with deep relationships in their everyday lives. The town is a "normal" place for them. Borderlanders, as legitimate actors, actively constitute the town's society even without legal recognition and precarious conditions.

Although I do not disregard the various imminent difficulties that they have to cope with in their everyday lives, I seek to adequately recognize their contribution to the border society in various sectors. It is too simplistic to criminalize them as people destroying society. An understanding of the town with this simplified notion is misleading. The town dominated by "illegal others" has much more complexities. Although social scientists have raised it before, the question regarding how societies/communities are potentially cohesive entities despite complex social and cultural relations remains highly relevant to understanding border communities/towns. In addressing this question, I use the border town of Mae Sot and its surroundings as the empirical site.

Background

<Map 2> Mae Sot District

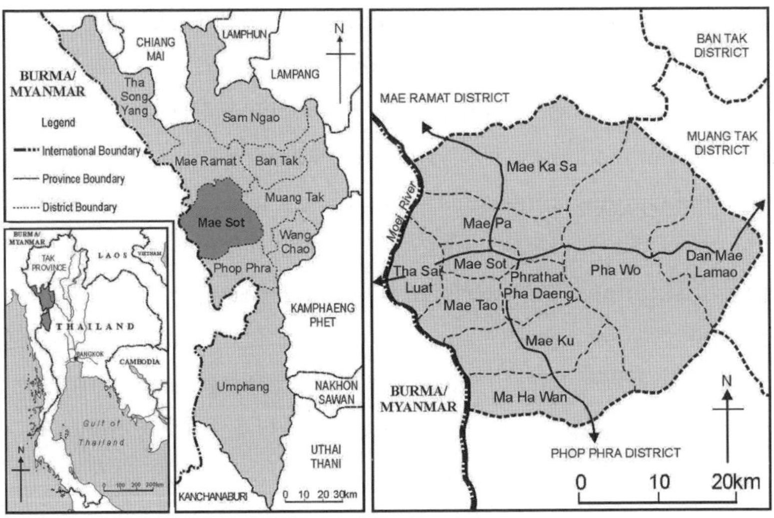

Mae Sot is located in the northwestern region of Thailand, 497 km from Bangkok, 87 km from Tak, 138 km from Mottama, and 425 km from Yangon. It borders Mae Ramat in the north, Phop Phra in the south, Muang Tak in the east, and Myawaddy, the Karen State of Myanmar in the west across the Moei River.

Mae Sot is in a flat valley formed by two mountain ranges -

the Thanon Thongchai mountain range and the Dawna mountain range. The former extends up from Chiang Mai Province and ends at Kanchanaburi Province, dividing Tak Province into two halves. The latter runs along the border between Thailand and Myanmar from the north of Karen State down to Tanintharyi Division. The rugged mountains of these ranges have permanently restricted communications between Mae Sot and the areas beyond the ranges. This feature, in turn, has contributed to Mae Sot's uniqueness in various sectors, such as population formation, culture, and economy, as we will see in the following chapters. Also, it was conducive to Mae Sot's central position in the western Tak Province, which also has the same geographical restrictions. Up from Tha Song Yang down to Umphang, for people in this region, Mae Sot is like a capital town where they pursue their livelihoods and education. Even when they go to Bangkok, they must stop in Mae Sot before continuing their journey because an extensive and convenient road over the mountain range is only connected to Mae Sot.[3]

Mae Sot historically played a linking role for traders traveling between the Indian Ocean and mainland Southeast Asia. The pre-modern kingdoms of Myanmar and Thailand used its position for military operations. It was a buffer area between these two archrivals throughout history. It is against this background that Mae Sot and its adjacent areas as "in-between" places accommodated various kinds of people, such as traders, fugitives, and ethnic traitors, even before

3 During my stay from July 2004 to July 2005, I visited a remote village in the southern part of Umphang District. Many residents were sending their children to secondary schools and a college in Mae Sot. Their commercial activities also centered on Mae Sot. I accompanied the Karen to take part in a ceremony for the establishment of a church in the village, known as Buangkhler.

the modern period.

Up until several decades ago, Mae Sot remained just a small village. When the Burmese military took power and introduced the Burmese Way to Socialism with her doors closed to the outside world from the early 1960s to the late 1980s, Mae Sot was a prominent entry point for the black markets along the Thailand-Myanmar border. The prolific operation of the black markets under the control of the Karen National Union (KNU) drew enormous attention from Thai locals as well as the ethnic Burmese who were seeking to eke out a livelihood. Specifically, the black markets gave rise to prominent local people in business who originated from other areas, particularly Bangkok. During the days of the operation of the black markets, in tandem with existing ethnic mixtures, Mae Sot saw the trend of domestic migration from other areas of Thailand to Mae Sot for border trade.

As the economic conditions of Myanmar were comparable to that of Thailand at this point,[4] the Burmese did not pursue economic opportunities in Thailand. Although the black markets operated near Mae Sot, since they primarily engaged in trade and transportation, they rarely sought permanent residence in Mae Sot.

However, conditions changed dramatically in the latter part of the 1980s. The Burmese economy fell to awful conditions, achieving the status of "Least Developed Country (LDC),"[5] while Thailand went through an enormous economic boom during the 1980s. A newly shaped Burmese military junta came to power and opened her long secluded doors to the outside countries. However, it kept a tight

4 For the economic conditions during 1962-88, see Myat Thein (2004: 85-120).

5 The details on LDC status will be shown in Chapter 2.

leash on domestic affairs, harshly trampled the democratic uprising, and penetrated the liberated areas held by ethnic rebels. The black markets were rendered obsolete in a series of assaults from the military regime, and the trading trend between both countries mostly took on official and formal ways.

Many Burmese migrants came to Mae Sot for their livelihood as the economic gap between Myanmar and Thailand widened during this period. Apart from economic migrants, political activists and refugees also flooded into the town and its outlying vicinities in search of refuge. To make matters more complex, the influx of refugees brought quite a few international agencies into the town. In the 1990s, dozens of international nongovernmental organizations (INGOs) opened their offices in Mae Sot to deliver humanitarian assistance. The United Nations High Commissioner for Refugees (UNHCR) also opened its field office in 1998.

Demographic expansion caused by the influx of alien people changed the economic and social conditions of the town. In the industrial sector, factories from other provinces relocated to the town to take advantage of cheap foreign labor. The number of factories increased from 118 in 1993 to 218 in 2000 (Maneepong 2002/2003: 91) and continued to evolve throughout the years to 400 as of 2014 (MAP Foundation and Clean Clothes Campaign 2014: 8). The number of registered Burmese factory workers also increased over the years: 3,708 in 1993, 4,716 in 1995, 6,735 in 1997, 14,793 in 2000, and 31,196 in 2005 (Mae Sot Labour Office 2005; Maneeong 2006: 14), 40,000 in 2010 and 64,395 as of 2016 (IOM 2016: 14). Unauthorized Burmese included, their number was estimated to be over 200,000 (Karen News 2016). Other economic sectors also saw a great deal of economic participation and contribution from them. It is widespread to find Burmese used in almost every shop in the town. The dominant presence of the Burmese is also observable in the realm of domestic work.

The presence of a sizeable number of Burmese brought Burmese socio-cultural elements into the town: they can watch Burmese television programs on cable channels; they maintain their indispensable habits of chewing betel, leaving so many "red spots" on many parts of the roads in the town; and they "kill time" by chatting and drinking tea in typical Burmese teashops which are found all over the town.

Moreover, they came to establish their own institutions. In education, schools for migrant children came into being with the help of migrant activists and foreign volunteers. Though limited, thousands of Burmese children learned Burmese school textbooks and English from foreigners. The migrant schools nurtured them as Burmese and global citizens to a certain degree.[6] In healthcare, they access a migrant clinic also established in collaboration with international partners, not necessarily relying on Thai healthcare institutions.

Migration also diversified the religious composition of the town. Besides Buddhism, the main religion among the majority of the Thais and the Burmese, other religions also became noticeable. One can see the prominent presence of Muslims in the town. Whereas Thai Muslims already existed, Burmese Muslim migrants increased the number of mosques in the town. Burmese ethnic groups such as

6 There are some cases of Burmese children in Mae sot who attended government schools in Myawaddy daily across the border.

the Chin and the Karen practiced Christianity. For example, those who engaged in KNU's activities were primarily Christian. Sikhs were noticeable among people in business who were Thai nationals. Apart from the religions mentioned above, many migrants retained animistic belief systems.

As a result of this considerable increase in otherness and illegality, the mode of societal formation had to be changed. "Otherness" is not necessarily despised but must be incorporated into society. Moreover, encountering modes between them and us also take on different ways. The integration of formality and informality significantly appears in the town's administration, economy, education, and cultural affairs.

In the next section, I will seek to elaborate upon my theoretical claims about understanding the town by critiquing some existing theories.

Quest for a Theoretical Framework

One conventional anthropological theme on Southeast Asian borders has centered on state formation in association with ethnic groups (e.g., Duncan 2008; Horstmann and Wadley 2006; Ishikawa 2010; Jonsson 2005; Keyes 1979; Scott 2009; Wijeyewardene *et al.* 1990). These studies have explored how states attempted to exert their influence on the borderlands and how the identities of those living across the borders took shape in interacting with states and other ethnic groups. These studies took place when nation-building projects stretched to remote border areas and thus focused on the influence of state penetration and the reaction of locals.

Currently, globalization and economic integration are transforming Southeast Asian borderlands. The Asian Development Bank, a notable player, and individual states have sought to exploit the borderlands to maximize economic interests (ADB 2001; 2004; Glassman 2010). Some scholarly works have reviewed this border project, focusing on its impact on localities and the reaction of local governments (Campbell 2018; Maneepong 2002/2003; 2004; 2005; Pitch 2007). Others explore the trade regulation of borderlands concerning local traders rather than state projects (Walker 1999) and social and cultural change in the age of globalization (e.g., Evans *et al.* 2002).

The study of the Thailand-Burma borderland epitomizes similar trends. However, in this borderland, the sizeable presence of ethnic rebellion groups, conflicts between the Burmese government and those groups, and the consequences of these conflicts, such as forced migration, have drawn the attention of scholars (Chiang 2002; Grundy-Warr 2004; Grundy-Warr and Wong 2002; Lang 2001; 2002; Lee 2001; Rajah 1990; 1994; Sharples 2020). Some academic and NGO reports deal with the lives of migrants in the border areas, including Mae Sot (Arnold 2004; 2006; Balčaitė 2019; BLSO 2002; Loong 2019; Reddy 2017; Thornton 2006; World Vision 2004).

A notable aspect of existing studies is that they intrinsically appeal to humanitarianism. One consequence is that we hardly see how migrants and refugees navigate their lives, relying on and using the border as a social world, despite the state's regulatory practices. I attempt to fill this gap, building upon some existing theoretical approaches deserving detailed discussion.

Plural Society

The situation described in Mae Sot parallels Furnivall's (1944; 1956) depiction of the "plural societies" of Burma and Indonesia, in which a plural society is defined as "a society, comprising two or more elements or social orders which live side by side, yet without mingling, in one political unit" (1944: 446). People in this society are divided into racial groups, and each group keeps its lifestyle separately, only meeting in the marketplace (1956: 304). It has been a critical concept for scholars to understand even the current post-colonial societies of the region.

The "plural society" was brought about by the migration of various ethnic groups - Chinese, Indian, and Europeans - into the colonies for economic development. According to Furnivall, these ethnic groups did not share everyday social demands on which a mature society should stand. Therefore, people in plural societies only pursue their economic gains without necessarily considering the welfare of society as a whole.

Although different conditions between the colonial and the modern period render direct comparisons implausible, it should not prevent the concept from being critically applied. It seems that what Furnivall had looked at was revisited: the diverse composition of ethnic groups - Thais, Burman, Karen, Mon, and Europeans - as a result of migration was conspicuous, and each group seemed to have its way of life, not combining with other ethnic groups. Residential areas are distinct, the types of labor are sectional, and clothes, food, and pastimes vary according to ethnic groups.

However, we can observe some inadequacies in applying Furnivall's concept to the town's situation. First, Furnivall's idea is too static because he assumes that society never experiences changes. At the outset of migration, the characteristics of the plural society, such as separate residence, sectional labor, and bounded culture, could be observed. However, as time passes, people will likely mix and integrate with others in various ways.

Second, Furnivall rigidly restricts contact points and social interaction to the marketplace. Wertheim (1980: 18) indicates that Furnivall denies any social and cultural contact between the different racial groups. He (1980:18) notes that a creolization process between immigrant groups was evident in the colonies. The creolization process must have happened in various everyday life fields. To assume that people only meet in the marketplace is too simplistic. We must consider social and cultural fields in understanding people's contacts.

Third, Furnivall dismisses the market's role in building relationships between racial groups. The market is not just a contact place but also a social field where diverse groups mingle, and inter-ethnic relationships occur. Rex (1980: 98), on the other hand, argues that the market draws people together into a single social system, produces new group affiliations, and gives new meaning to old ones.

Last, the problem in attempting to apply Furnivall's plural society model is that we cannot clearly understand the roles of states in forming society. Furnivall does not delve into the role of states in maintaining society, apart from the role the state plays as an initial cause for the engendering of a plural society by bringing various groups of people into society. It seems that colonial states maintained the *status quo* with a reluctant attitude to the favorable resolution of the plural society. However, in the post-colonial period, nation-states, in the nation-building process, directly intervene in the affairs of society through policies and state apparatus such as the bureaucracy. Especially in border areas, this aspiration of states is manifest, regardless of whether it is efficient, since borders are considered the utmost markers of state sovereignty. This final point regarding the role of states hardly finds a position in Furnivall's discussion. Thus, we need a theoretical framework that positions/ accounts for states' influence in explaining society formation.

State-Society Approaches

State-society approaches provide viewpoints to explain how state and society contest to implement the interests of each other. These approaches challenge both state-centric approaches and community-confined approaches. The state-centric approaches presuppose a center-periphery dichotomy and are preoccupied with center dominance over the periphery. In these approaches, peripheries are predestined to be incorporated into political, economic, and cultural centers. Modernization theories (e.g., Inkeles 1969; Rostow 1960), dependency theories (e.g., Frank 1969), and world systems theories (e.g., Wallerstein 1979) take on this assumption. This center-periphery model has been prominent not only in discussions of modern societies but also analyses of pre-colonial social formation in Southeast Asia (Walker 1999: 6). Phrases such as "mandala" (Wolters 1999) and "galactic polity" (Tambiah 1976) presuppose the asymmetrical power relationships and radiance effects of influence from centers. Although these state/center-centric approaches are informative in understanding the nature of the centers' power and aspects of their influence in peripheries, they oversimplify power relations (Walker 1999: 8). They show a lack of interest in the impact of the periphery on the center (Migdal 1988: xv).

On the other hand, community-confined approaches tend to assume that communities have their modes of life without much consideration of external forces that act upon them. In other words, community-centered studies regard their fields as microcosms without outside influences such as states. As Migdal mentions (1988: xvi), these studies, while occasionally referring to state policies and resources, often remain enmeshed in the intricacies of social life at the local level.

In sum, both center-periphery and community-centered models do not shed light on understanding the complexities of the local, which state-society approaches attempt to overcome. State-society approaches depict society as a *mélange* of social organizations comprising two facets; first, groups are heterogeneous both in their form and in the rules they apply; second, the distribution of social control in society may be diffused among numerous, relatively autonomous groups rather than mainly concentrated in the state (Migdal 1988: 28). It suggests that "focusing on these struggles within society, between states and other social organizations such as clans, tribes, language groups, and the like, will give new insights into the processes of social and political change" (Migdal 1988: 31). The image coming to my mind when dealing with the approaches, is "a strenuous tug of war" where players are persistent not to lose a rope. The two opposing teams in the game are "society" and "state," while the "rope" represents resources. In order to gain more and not lose an inch of resources, the games the teams play tend to be tense. The game image vividly explains each team's relentless aspiration to secure and acquire societal dominance.

In state-society theories, it is assumed that the boundaries between state and society are sharply drawn. Though later theoretical developments saw the various patterns of relationships between state and society, paying particular attention to collaborations between them (Migdal 1998; 2001; Dauvergne 1998), the inherent and essential assumptions of the theories are conflicts and tensions between two extreme forces. Therefore, in this model, patterns of behaviors and relationships such as "accommodation," "negotiation," and "unofficial/informal actions" do not draw much attention as compared to conflict-centered ones.

Moreover, as the theories mainly deal with cases within national boundaries, it does not provide a clear understanding of elusive cases in border areas. This model does not attempt to comprehend the impact of external factors such as cross-border movements and illegal society members in borderlands. Especially in the case of Mae Sot, where the number of alien people who are mostly illegally staying is enormously predominant, rigid application of the theories cannot provide adequate accounts of societal formation.

Globalization

At this juncture, it seems cliché to introduce debates of globalization on whether states are in decline and whether a borderless world has arrived. Whether we agree with Ohmae (1990; 1995), who makes a bold claim about the demise of states, or whether we are inclined to hear the persistent roles of states in authorizing the movements of capital and people (Panitch 1996), we can find the debates revolving around "borders" and the degree of their openness. In other words, the issue of borders has been the dominant theme in the discourses of globalization, regardless of theoretical positions. We have witnessed common-sense assumptions of borders as important markers against neighboring states have become problematized. The traditional understanding of space tied to the notions of disconnectedness and boundedness cannot grasp happenings in and across borders.

Conventional anthropological research assumes that the modes of natives' lives were formed and maintained in a particular place, hardly considering relationships with and influences from outside. Advocates of globalization theories (e.g., Appadurai 1996; Gupta and Ferguson 1997) have criticized that traditional anthropological notions dealt with a particular place as discrete, separate, and self-reliant. These approaches tended to spatially incarcerate natives to a particular place (Appadurai 1996), taking for granted the isomorphism of peoples, places, and cultures (Gupta and Ferguson 1997: 34).

Scholars that interrogate the relevance of this traditional approach suggest that we now need to look at the mobile features of people's modes of life in the era of globalization. Therefore, in new approaches, "migrants" and "refugees" are considered normal subjects, showing the very nature of their mobility. Also, scholars pay special attention to borderlands, suggesting that "the notion of borderlands is a more adequate conceptualization of the 'normal' locale of the postmodern subject, rather than dismissing them as insignificant, as marginal zones, thin slivers of land between stable places" (Gupta and Ferguson 1997: 48).

In the anthropological globalization approaches, borderlands also play the role of a "node" in interconnecting national boundaries

(Hannerz 1996: 17). Hannerz (1996: 67) notes,

> The interconnectedness typically takes the shape of a relatively continuous spectrum of interacting meanings and meaningful forms, along which the various contributing historical sources of the culture are differentially visible and active. The context of center-periphery relationships suggests both the spatial dimension and the fact that the creole continuum has a built-in political economy of culture. Social power and material resources, as well as prestige, tend to be matched with the spectrum of cultural forms. At one end of this continuum there is thus the culture of the center, with greater although not always unambiguous prestige, as in creolist linguistics the "Standard," the "superstratum." At the other end are the cultural forms of the farthest periphery, often in greater parochial variety. In between are, to put it simply, a variety of mixtures.

In this interconnectedness, borderlands are not considered to be dominated by the center as conventional center-periphery approaches argue. Instead, these are where interplay and mixtures or creolization between the center and the periphery occur. Absolute distinctions between "we" and the distant "they" are blurred, and "transnational" characteristics can be observed (Kearney 1991: 55).

Though connectedness and creolization are very informative concepts in comprehending current phases occurring in borderlands, we need to ask whether these are "new" traits that have only occurred recently, especially when considering the Thailand-Myanmar borderland. People have been moving and migrating for a long time. Even in the wake and development of nation-states and national boundaries, the borderland was relatively porous, so cross-border movements were not heavily restricted. Historical factors and geographical features play enduring roles, leading to the creation of mixtures and the creolization of society in the borderland. Theories of globalization do not seem to pay due attention to this point. Recent development may be a little exaggerated.

Another point that globalization theorists dismiss is the issue of power. Walker (1999: 11-12) indicates that connections and flows in borderland areas are not haphazardly taking place but are regulated. He goes on to argue that liberalizing initiatives that encourage mobility and passage should not be assumed to be initiatives that undermine regulatory power. Instead, these create the conditions for a new mix of regulatory practices (1999: 15). He defines "regulation" as "the practices people employ to initiate and control mobility and interconnection" (1999: 12). He does not restrict the agencies that hold the legitimacy in regulating practices to states. According to him (1999: 13), private interest groups (border traders in his case) also participate in various ways to regulate actions.

However, though he denies the monopoly of regulating practices by the state, the concept inherently connotes disciplinary actions which make the subordinates conform to regulations laid down by power holders. Therefore, even though he notes some collaboration between frontier communities and the state in the operation of border trades (1999: 111-112), this suggestion is not quite adequately positioned in his critical arguments that the state still controls borders. While his attempts to counteract triumphant proclamations of borderless worlds or liberalizing borders by ultra-globalization theorists are meaningful, these attempts have led him to emphasize the notions of state-centric regulation rather than give a balanced understanding of borderlands. Therefore, though the cases and realities in his book show various relationships between the state and border communities, including negotiations and collaborations as well as tensions and conflicts, we only get *ad hoc* explanations of such cases within the stringent conceptual framework of "regulation."

The critical question we must raise is not whether the state is losing or maintaining control in borderlands and societies. This question only succeeds in giving tautological answers that validate the presence of the state in borderlands. This question is intrinsically limited in understanding the complexities of borderlands where the ebb and flow of people are continuously occurring, and the informal/unofficial is deep-rooted. Attempts at understanding the situations in borderlands demand a new framework where these features should be incorporated.

Towards a Border Social System

I seek to understand the border town and the formation of the society with the concept of a "border social system." Before dealing with it, it is necessary to identify what a "social system" is. Parsons and Giddens are two prominent scholars seeking to define the concept.[7]

Parsons (1991 [1951]: 25) mentions,

> Since a social system is a system of processes of

7 For scholars' definitions of the concept, see Bailey (1994).

> interaction between actors, it is the structure of the relations between the actors as involved in the interactive process which is essentially the structure of the social system. The system is a network of such relationships.

According to Giddens (1979: 65-66),

> Social systems involve regularized relations of interdependence between individuals or groups, that typically can be best analysed as *recurrent social practices*. Social systems are systems of social interaction (emphasis original).

The key words in defining the concept are "interaction" and "relations" between actors. A social system is not randomly constituted but based on recurrent practices. The concept of a social system can be applied to the study of borderlands. Unlike the assumption made in the concept of a plural society, interactions and relationships between actors take place on a recurrent basis in the border town. A social system is observable there.

What makes the difference between understanding social and border social systems? In the former, actors tend to be formal, legal, and rational. Scholars analyzing a particular social system do not pursue to interrogate the movements and impacts of informal or unauthorized forces on society to a considerable degree.

In contrast, understanding a border social system is incomplete without accommodating the constant ebb and flow of people, money, and idea, though unauthorized. The early functionalists such as Parsons are criticized for dismissing the dynamics and changes in society at the expense of overly focusing on "equilibrium" and "stability" (Bailey 1994; Giddens 1984; Leach (1964 [1954]). Border social systems show dynamic changes that are an intrinsic part of the border society. Alvarez (1984: 121) states, "[A] social system or society is built upon organized, fluid movement of people through time and space." He (1984: 121-122) goes on to mention,

> [R]ather than viewing the frequency of movement and the volume of population movements as disturbances to a system and a departure from its rules, fluid personnel are the lifeblood of societies. Migration and mobility (flow) are an organized part of these social systems...... the flow of people through a continuing migration (legal, undocumented, temporary, permanent, circular, and so on) is built into the fabric of border society.

The patterns of interaction between actors in borderlands differ from typical social systems. The presence of unauthorized actors brings about different types of interaction beyond conventional understanding. Not only are there formal/regulated ways of relationships, but informal patterns of interaction are pretty prominent.

Though a "border social system" may sound like just a literal mixture between "border" and "social system," however, its physical base, the border, plays a decisive role in producing a different kind of society in terms of actors, mobility, and interaction. Illegal/undocumented people play legitimate roles in a border social system, the constant flow of people, money, and ideas across borders does not necessarily disturb social formation, and informal relationships are noticeable to a great degree.

I argue that understanding borderlands is incomplete without paying attention to formal and informal integration. In proposing the necessity of dealing with the informal economy, Hinton (2000: 22-23) critiques conventional ways of approaching the economy with two points. First, in developing countries, the informal sector comprises a substantial portion of total production. Therefore, "to omit it from calculations builds in significant distortions" (2000: 22). Second, to make a sharp distinction between the two is invalid because they are intertwined in complex ways. He states that much of the cross-border trade would fall into the informal sector in mainland Southeast Asia. According to him (2000: 23), it is not only the trade in heroin and narcotics that takes on informal ways, but the activities of a myriad of small traders are subsumed under the "black economy."

Tannenbaum and Durrenberger (1990: 283) also make similar arguments, mentioning that the "'formal' and 'informal' are not economic facts. They are categories relevant not to the working of economic systems, but to government measurement policies." Moreover, according to them (1990: 283), "what is formal in one country may be informal in another; what is informal at one time may be formal at another. These are cultural categories, not economic facts."

Abraham and Van Schendel (2005: 4) problematize the state categorization of the legal and the illegal. They suggest that though many transnational movements of people, commodities, and ideas are illegal in the state understanding, they are pretty acceptable and licit/legitimate in the eyes of participants in these transactions and flows. Thus, it is imperative to consider these illegal aspects of cross-border movement to understand the border economy holistically.

The need to consider the informal sector is not confined to the economy but extended to other sectors. Especially in the case of Mae Sot, where Burmese political activists and international relief agencies take prominent residence with their political and relief structures, the administration and governance of the town take a different form. Alongside the state administrative regime, other regimes, such as those headed by political activists, are also in operation in the town. Governance in the town includes these non-state regimes. Unauthorized Burmese make their lives under the governance.

In the education sector of the town, the informal is also evidently observable. The fact that more than thirty informal migrant schools encompass several thousand migrant students in Mae Sot vividly shows the strong presence of the informal. State education authorities must deal with these informal migrant schools, not necessarily attempting to destroy them.

To understand the cultural fields in the town, one requires an integrating approach of the formal and informal. Certain levels of creolization occur in the town in festivals, food, and languages. Though most of them are illegal residents, the Burmese actively participate in cultural events. Thus, neglecting those illegal residents just because of their lack of legal status does not provide an adequate explanation to understand the cultural aspects of the border town.

The book demonstrates how "others"[8] are integrated into the

8 The Burmese are the only components of "others." Other ethnic groups, such as the Chinese and the Muslims, are included in "others" too. "Otherness" in the book means some traits or natures that non-Thai ethnic people construct. Since the Burmese are major others in Mae Sot, this book treats the Burmese as main others.

border social system in Mae Sot and its vicinities. I argue that the border social system builds upon interactions or relationships among actors, including unauthorized people and that these interactions take place in a way that integrates the informal/unofficial and the formal/official. The informal or the illegal does not necessarily destroy societal formation but significantly constitutes the town's society.

My proposal of the border social system counteracts and overcomes *homo sacer* or bare life thesis that has drawn scholars' attention concerning migrant/refugee lives (Agamben 1998; De Genova 2002; 2013; Derks 2013; Pattana 2014; Phianphachong 2018; Rajaram and Grundy-Warr 2004). These scholars often regard the border as an exceptional space where the state exercises a sovereign power, which renders migrants' lives bare and precarious without protection. I differ from them in that I consider the border a possible space that provides migrants with various resources to overcome the state of bare lives. The border facilitates migrants to imagine a new possibility, practice mobility, and craft their life trajectories, navigating through legal and illegal domains. Migrants are a legitimate part of the border social system.

Long Journey

The field research in Mae Sot and its adjacent areas spanned almost two decades. My first was in December 1999. Then I stayed in Mae La camp between February and April 2000, intending to deal with the adaptation and identities of the Karen refugees for my master's thesis. I returned in December 2003 and spent a couple of weeks mainly in Mae Sot with a visit to the refugee Camp. My purpose was to re-contact former informants and arrange for later full-scale research for my doctoral thesis. During that time, I noticed many changes to my former informants' lives and Mae Sot's landscape. Many of them were now staying in Mae Sot, where alien people's presence became more prominent than before. Therefore, I turned my research focus from "genuine" refugees inside refugee camps to border issues with an expanded research framework.

I conducted full-scale year-round field research from July 2004 to July 2005 as visiting fellow at the Institute of Asian Studies, Chulalongkorn University. During this time, I primarily stayed in Mae Sot. However, I frequently visited Mae La camp and went to Umphang District areas, located south of Tak Province, to compare with Mae Sot. I conducted follow-up research in December 2005 before completing my doctoral thesis. My visits continued almost every year during the 2010s to catch up with changing situations in the face of regional integration and subsequent development projects. However, the Coronavirus pandemic prevented me from continuing my endeavors in the early part of the 2020s.

During my stay in Mae Sot, I mainly associated with a group of Karen people centering on a church. Through them, I approached the Karen and inter-ethnic Burmese organizations. At the level of grassroots research, such as studying the living conditions of migrant workers, I was able to gain access to them with the assistance of some Karen church members who were also living amongst them. Though the Karen people in Mae Sot, especially the Christian Karen, seemed to have their lifestyles, they were also part of a broad migrant people. Therefore, my association with them was an entry point into the lives of other migrant people living with and around them. Through them, I was also able to investigate how connections between the migrant population and camp refugees were maintained and how cross-border movements of their relatives and their goods took place.

In the beginning, it was a big challenge to approach government sectors such as the district office, the municipal office, the customs office, the immigration office, and the labor office because they could consider much of my topic concerning illegal or unauthorized people and organizations sensitive. The state apparatuses officially did not allow them to be present in the town. In this respect, I needed someone that guaranteed my status in introducing me to those offices. It was very fortuitous for me to rent a house from a landlord - a prominent businessman who was in very close contact with these offices and also a member of the Tak Chamber of Commerce. Throughout my stay, he consistently helped me contact them for interviews. Besides, I acquired much information on the border economy through his cross-border trade experience. Also, with my informant's assistance, I participated in several meetings, activities, and social gatherings organized by local businessmen.

As time passed, I built friendships with some young local businessmen who ran shops, operated factories, and engaged in border trade in the town and its vicinities. Close socialization with them enabled me to look at the town's economic situation not from official statements but from real experiences on the ground. I also established close relationships with other Thai locals by participating in various social gatherings such as football matches, festivals, funerals, and wedding ceremonies. Through these social relationships, I witnessed how Thai locals' lives were associated with others in their mundane everyday lives.

One interesting point that differentiates the town from other border towns is the noticeable presence of international parties, including the UNHCR and INGOs, mainly concerned with refugees. Though the number of people working there was small, they dealt with hundreds of thousands of people in and around the town, and their influence was never negligible. In approaching these international organizations, I received preponderant assistance from the Karen working in INGOs and the UNHCR. It was not uncommon that the Karen, whether from Burma or Thailand, were the majority of workers in these organizations due to their ability to speak Karen and English, which are essential for dealing with refugees and foreigners. I frequently visited some NGOs and sometimes followed them to a refugee camp to observe their activities. Moreover, my wife's involvement as a special education teacher in an NGO brought me many favors. I was more accessible to refugee camps, observing the day-to-day operations of INGOs and participating in those organizations' social gatherings along with her.

Most of the information I draw in this book comes from participant observation, informal conservations, and formal interviews. I used the first two methods for the focal groups, such as a group of Karen Church members and local friends, and the last for interviewing personnel from government offices and ethnic or Burmese political organizations.

In the initial phase, I attempted to use the survey distribution method to understand the general conditions of migrant people. Indeed, I employed this method a couple of times. However, I sensed that some people feared their details would be revealed and end up in the hands of Thai officials. Therefore, I decided not to use the method.

The diversity of the border society is evident in the list of my informants, which includes unauthorized migrants, smugglers, business tycoons, customs officials, the head officer (*nay ampoe*) of the district, people in ethnic organizations, Western NGO workers, and UNHCR officials. Their diverse voices inspired me to attempt to understand the particular place as holistically as possible.

The long journey was a learning process where I realized how people in precarious conditions live by overcoming those difficulties. It is part of my appreciation of them to locate their legitimate presence in the border social system.

Outline of the Book

Following this introductory chapter, Chapter 2 traces the historical formation of the border social system. It discusses that the migration of various groups, notably from Myanmar, engendered the formation of the society in the town throughout history. Particularly the multitudinous migration since the late 1980s transformed the town so that it came to accommodate unauthorized others to sustain the social system.

Chapter 3 examines Burmese migrant enclaves in conjunction with governance, mobility, and connectivity. The chapter demonstrates that mobility and connectivity are catalysts in forming migrant enclaves as transnational conjunctural spaces. In the migrants' constant pursuit of better lives, enclaves facilitate their passage from Myanmar through Mae Sot to Bangkok and other countries.

Chapter 4 highlights behind-the-scenes informal economic activities focusing on unauthorized riverbank Burmese merchants, the cross-border movement of goods, and the nexus of ethnic politics and border trade. The chapter shows that although the state labels unauthorized trade smuggling, it is *withi chiwit*, a "way of life" for Burmese merchants. It further demonstrates that the ordering of the border is not entirely regulated by state agencies but by other social groups, notably ethnic groups.

Chapter 5 chapter examines migrant schools. Their substantial existence enables migrant children to have their education without proper legal status. The growth of migrant schools marked the building of a migrant education institution in cooperation with international partners, showing progress in the constitution of migrant lives. This chapter shows the impressive growth of the migrant education institution, bringing the state into play and having achieved a certain level of recognition from the state as a legitimate formal institution.

Chapter 6 scrutinizes how a Burmese migrant clinic town cares for migrant patients and activates cross-border healthcare mobility. Since the late 1980s, the clinic has developed its capacity and serves as a prominent healthcare institution across the border. Despite its illegality, Thai authorities recognize its importance and collaborate with the clinic. The study reveals that collaborations with various partners play essential roles in the constitution of the clinic. Partnerships with multiple individuals and organizations have empowered the clinic to undertake a unique position in the border society. The legitimate presence of the migrant clinic in the border town mediates and strengthens their transnational mobility across the border.

Chapter 7 explores how the forces of mobility affect the border society. In particular, it examines two forces generating population movements involving Burmese migrants: the Bangkok dream, which pushes migrants from the borderland to Bangkok in their search for better opportunities, and refugee resettlement programs, which take refugees from the borderland to other countries. These two processes create massive human migrations across and beyond the border, with Mae Sot as a node.

Chapter 8 summarizes the previous chapters and suggests how the book's findings contribute to a general understanding of borderlands.

Chapter 2

The Development of a Border Social System

Introduction

Anthony Reid's eminent attempts (1988; 1993) to uncover "collective destinies" in which geography formed commonalities in people's lives in the history of Southeast Asia can be applied to the case of Mae Sot. As briefly mentioned in the previous chapter, Mae Sot, located between Myanmar and Thailand, and in the broader context the ocean and the mainland, has served as a buffer and node throughout history. Mae Sot had collective destinies influenced by the political and economic development of the region.

Against the backdrop of this geographical formation, this chapter reveals that commerce and war are the prominent factors in the development of the social system in the borderland. In the face of political and economic developments in the region, Mae Sot and its adjacent areas as "in-between" places accommodated various kinds of people, such as traders, fugitives, and ethnic traitors, even before the modern period. Above all, turbulent incidents during the pre-modern period, such as ethnic conflicts between the Burman and the Mon/Karen and Thai-Burmese warfare, drove people in lower Myanmar to the borderland around Mae Sot. Similarly, the British colonization and post-colonial ethnic insurgent movements and massive operation of black markets affected the flow of people and population movement and the expansion of settlement in the border town. The current cross-border movement of people has taken on this historical trajectory.

In tracing the town's settlement history, this chapter divides it into four periods: first, from the beginning to the 1820s; second, from the 1820s to 1962; third, from 1962 to 1988; and last, from 1988 to now. In each period, commerce and political conflicts engendered population movement and the subsequent development of border society. Mae Sot brought various groups of traders, such as Mon merchants in the Sukhothai period, Chinese caravans during the British colonization of Myanmar, and black market merchants during the period of "Burmese Way to Socialism." Meanwhile, Mae Sot accommodated the Mon and Karen refugees and fugitives during the Toungoo and Konbaung dynasties and the political insurgents of the Burmese students and the Karen at present.

The constant ebb and flow of people is a conspicuous but normal phenomenon in the borderland. Fluid people are core elements of the border society. Fluidity does not necessarily destabilize the social system in the borderland; instead, it is an inherent nature of the border society. The history of Mae Sot shows that the flows of various groups of people, most of whom were affected by commerce and war, engendered the society. The following sections will touch on the fluid movements of these people associated with developing the social system in the Thailand-Myanmar borderland.

From Passages to Sanctuary: From the Beginning to the 1820s

Commercial Connections

The first historical record of the existence of Mae Sot occurred in the earlier period of Sukhothai. During the reigns of Ramkhamhaeng's father (around the 1270s), a ruler of Muang Chot called Khun Samchon invaded Sukhothai's western outpost at Tak. Some scholars assume Muang Chot to be Mae Sot (Anurak 1998; Coedès 1968: 349; Sunait 1990: 274; Wyatt 2004: 41). Ramkhamhaeng defeated the forces of Muang Chot, and placed it under the rule of Sukhothai. During Ramkhamhaeng's reign, Sukhothai experienced geographical expansion, including Mae Sot, as indicated in the inscription of Ramkhamhaeng.

> The places whose submission he received on the east include Sraluang, Song Khwae [Phitsanulok], Lumbacai, both banks of the Mekong up to Vientiane. To the south Khanthi, Phrabang [Nakhon Sawan], Phraek [Chainat], Suphanburi, Ratchaburi, Phetchaburi and [Nakhon] Si Thammarat as far as the coast of the ocean. Westwards, *Chot* [*Mae Sot*],…n [Pan near Martaban] and Hangsaphadi [Hamsawati, Pegu], ending at the sea. To the north, Phlae [Phrae], Man, N…[Nan], Phlua [Pua] and across the Mekong as far as Java [Luang Prabang] (emphasis added) (Terwiel 2002: 12).

As shown above, the reigning areas of Sukhothai reached the coastal areas of the Indian Ocean, such as Mottama (Martaban) and Bago (Pegu), where the Mon settlement was predominant and with which Mae Sot had commercial connections. The story of Wareru,[9] born at Thaton to a Shan father and a Mon mother, testifies to this fact. He was in the habit of visiting the Siamese capital of Sukhothai for trading purposes and had settled in Sukhothai. While he was there, he eventually ascended to a high position in the palace as a captain to the guards of King Ramkhamhaeng. Interestingly,

9 His mon name is Magadu (Htin Aung 1967: 78) and Thai sources record his name as Chao Fa Rua (Coedès 1968: 209)

he commenced a love affair with one of the king's daughters and persuaded her to elope to his original place. Settling down in Mottama, he participated in a series of intriguing incidents against the Burmese governor. Becoming a rebellion leader, he captured Mottama and Bago. By 1287, he had gained control over the entire country south of Pyay (Prome) and Toungoo. Wareru placed his new kingdom under the overlordship of Sukhothai (Coedès 1968: 209-210; Hall 1981: 179; Halliday 1917: 10-11; Harvey 1967: 110-111; Htin Aung 1967: 78-80; Terwiel 2002: 14).

Though the name Mae Sot does not appear in the story, it can be easily assumed that Mae Sot was definitely included in the journeys of Wareru between Mottama and Sukhothai. Also, the fact that Wareru was once a merchant vindicated the commercial connection between these two places through the passage of Mae Sot. The findings of Sukhothai style ceramics and Chinese style ones in the adjacent areas of Mae Sot also attested that Mae Sot linked these two places and in the broader context between the Indian Ocean and inland areas including China (Grave 1995; Rau and Hughes 1985; Spinks 1956). Indeed, this connection between Mae Sot and lower Myanmar had existed long before the Sukhothai period. Hall (1981 [1954]: 24) mentions that since the time of Southeast Asian proto-history, one of the overland trade routes was via the Mawlamyine (Moulmein) and Rahaeng (Tak) passes,[10] where Mae Sot was included. Apart from commerce, religion also linked Mae Sot with the mainland and the ocean. Monks in Sukhothai made long journeys

10 Tak was under the influence of the northern Thai kingdom of Chiang Mai in the eighteenth century and was known as Rahaeng. When central Thai, Ayutthaya, took over in that century, they substituted the even older name, Tak, which could date from as far as the time of the Ramkhamhaeng inscription (Renard 1980b: 27).

traveling overland to Mottama, from which they embarked upon the long sea voyage to Sri Lanka (Frasch 2002: 65f; Terwiel 2002: 15). All in all, the historical records show that during the Sukhothai period Mae Sot was once populated[11] and played a linking role between the ocean and the mainland for commercial and religious purposes.

As mentioned earlier, the situation of lower Myanmar greatly impacted the development of Mae Sot. Lower Myanmar kept being a reference point for the development of Mae Sot. Maritime trade expanded in lower Myanmar at the outset of the age of commerce, the mid-fifteenth century (Reid 1993: 13). Although the coastal areas of Myanmar experienced an increase of maritime trade in the eleventh century (Frasch 2002: 64), it was "in the age of commerce" that lower Myanmar witnessed a great leap of trade in connection with other parts of Southeast Asia.[12]

Lieberman also elaborated on this connection between lower Myanmar and other parts of Southeast Asia. He (1980: 205) explains that the maritime centers in lower Myanmar, such as Pathein (Bassein), Bago, Mottama, and Ye, benefited from the expansion of the Indian Ocean and Indonesian commerce. Lieberman (1980: 205) observes that "in the mid-fifteenth century not only the volume of trade passing through the Mon ports expand in absolute terms, but the relative importance of the Mon area as a link in the Asian trade

11 The Lawa are said to be the earliest settlers in Northwestern Thailand including adjacent areas of Mae Sot (Condominas 1990; Srisakra 1986).

12 Aung-Thwin (2002) argues that in general, the application of "the age of commerce" in the case of Myanmar is not appropriate since the centers of the Burmese kingdoms were located in upper Myanmar which had placed more importance on the production of agriculture. However, the case of lower Myanmar should be dealt with differently from that of upper Myanmar. Throughout its history, much of the development of lower Myanmar was heavily dependent on commerce.

network increased." Commerce in lower Myanmar consists of three principal components (Lieberman 1980: 206; 1984: 27): the first was the trade with the rising center of Malacca and north Sumatra, the second line of commerce was with West Asia and India, particularly Gujarat, the Coromandel Coast, and Bengal, and the third segment was the inland commerce line between the eastern ports of Mottama and Siam. It was evident that Mae Sot played a linking role in the case of the third component.

The new port of Ye (south of Mottama) opened in 1438 to accommodate the expansion of trade volume in lower Myanmar (Reid 1993: 13). The shipyards of Mottama supplied many of the biggest junks for the merchants from other parts of Southeast Asia such as Malacca, Java and even south China, because Mottama was best placed to access large stands of Burmese teak (Reid 1993: 42).

The Portuguese capture of Malacca in 1511 further enhanced the commercial position of lower Myanmar. To escape Portuguese interference, merchants took alternative routes to lower Myanmar. The ports of lower Myanmar facilitated their transpeninsular trade with the Gulf of Siam. Moreover, the newly emergent anti-Portuguese centers of Aceh and Banten began to provide lower Myanmar with Eastern commodities to draw the attraction of Indian merchants reluctant to make the long journey to the Malay/Indonesian ports (Lieberman 1984: 28). This series of economic development convinced us that groups of merchants passed through Mae Sot in their journeys between lower Myanmar and inland Southeast Asia.

Warfare and Refugees

The economic proliferation of lower Myanmar induced

confrontations between the Burmese and the Siamese. The two sides attempted to secure lower Myanmar and enter into flourishing trade, which resulted in warfare between them. At first, Ayutthaya subjugated Tanintharyi (Tenasserim) in the 1460s and Dawei (Tavoy) in 1488 to obtain direct trade opportunities via the Indian Ocean in an attempt to overcome the limited access to Malacca and placed the region under its control until the mid-sixteenth (Sunait 2002: 19-20; Wyatt 2004: 72-73). However, Tabinshwehti of Toungoo captured Bago in 1539 and subsequently moved his palace there, hoping to engage in maritime trade. He also conquered Mottama in 1541 and subsequently placed lower Myanmar, which had been under the influence of Ayutthaya with the tributary status, under his control (Harvey 1967: 154-155; Lieberman 1984: 29-30; Wyatt 2004: 77). Two kingdoms were on the brink of battle. In late 1548, Tabinshwehti mobilized all his armies, including Burmese and Mon soldiers and Portuguese mercenaries, to commence war against Ayutthaya. During this military expedition, Burmese armies started from Mottama, crossed the Three Pagoda Pass, and reached Kanburi (Kanchanaburi) on the distant periphery of Ayutthaya. However, in the later military operation of 1563, the armies passed through the route between Mottama and Tak called the Rahaeng route or *dan* Mae Lamao (Mae Lamao customs station). From Mottama, the route led to the village of Taphu along a river. From there, the armies marched overland, crossing the Moei River at Myawaddy and Mae Sot until they reached the Mae Ping River opposite Rahaeng village, where the provincial district of Tak (Muang Tak) is located at the present day. Damrong (2001: 15-16) mentions that this was the usual route taken by the people of the northern provinces of Siam.

In Siamese history, it was called "the road to the outpost and duty station of Mae Lamao," which is currently one of the villages in Mae Sot District (Damrong 2001: 15-16; Pamaree 2005a: 79-81).

Perennial battles and rebellions in lower Myanmar engendered the displacement of people throughout history. In order to regain control of Ayutthaya, many Mon and Thai ethnic war captives in lower Myanmar were forced to join Toungoo's protracted military expeditions. Due to the insufferable condition, Mon and Tai war captives repeatedly rose in rebellion and fled away from lower Myanmar towards Siamese areas (Pamaree 2005b: 12-13). Mountains around Mae Sot provided hiding places for these fugitives and refugees. As James Scott (2009) mentions, the hills were the zones of refuge for the people evading from valley states. The early settlement in Mae Sot was associated with this movement of fugitives and refugees.

Though Ayutthaya fell and became a vassal state of Toungoo in 1569, achieving independence did not take long. Subsequently, by 1600, it claimed Tanintharyi and Dawei again to regain direct access to maritime trade with the Indian Ocean. However, Toungoo moved its capital from Bago to Inwa (Ava) in 1636 and posted governors in Bago and Mottama. Harvey (1967: 193) mentions that this capital relocation was due to the failures of the attempted coalescence with the Talaings (Mon). The rebellions of the Mon in lower Myanmar culminated in the fall of Toungoo in the 1750s. Alaunghpaya quelled the Mon uprisings and turned his attention to Siam. Like in the earlier days, full-scale wars between the two kingdoms ensued. In this warfare between Konbaung and Siam, the Mottama-Tak route, where the Mae Sot route was situated, was again used for military expeditions. The 1785 expedition which attacked Bangkok took this route as part of a five-pronged attack.[13] The Burmese armies most probably began their journey from Mottama to Tak by passing through Myawaddy and Mae Sot. Then they marched southward to Bangkok (Pamaree 2005b: 19).

The Mon were continuously summoned as levies in the series of military expeditions. They eventually mutinied in 1773, devastated Yangon, and in fear of retaliation, migrated to Siam with their families (Harvey 1967: 259). In 1814, another rebellion by the Mon in Mottama culminated in a refugee influx into Siam (Halliday 1913: 5).

Lieberman (1978; 1984: 218-219) mentions that the Mon were not the only group behind these insurgencies in lower Myanmar. Instead, many other ethnic groups, notably the Karen, joined the uprisings. The leader of the 1740 uprising in Mottama, Smin Dhaw, was Karen. Along with the Mon, the Karen in lower Myanmar were in prolonged turmoil between the 1740s and 1820s. Most obviously, many Karen communities lay along the routes through which the various armies passed. Many of the Karen were forced to provide provisions, recruited as guides and spies, and taken as captives (Keyes 1979: 34-35; Renard 1980b: 15). Due to the series of turbulent situations, they migrated to Siam along with the Mon in search of refuge. Since then, Siamese historical records began to deal with the Karen as a significant ethnic element (Keyes 1979: 45; Renard 1980a: 131).

---

13 Bodowphaya led the invasion of Bangkok in 1785. The five directions whereby he remarkably stormed Siam are as follows: 1) from Myeik (Mergui) to Chumphon and Chaiya southwardly; 2) From Dawei to Ratburi, Phetburi to meet up with the force at Chumphon; 3) Three Pagoda Pass to Kanchanaburi, then directly against Bangkok; 4) from Mottama to Tak and Kamphaengphet; and 5) from Chiang Saen to Lampang and southeastward to Phisanulok (Pamaree 2005b: 19).

There were three routes by which the fugitives traveled on their way to refuge in Siam. Mottama was their central rallying point. From there, they took the northern pass via Myawaddy, Mae Sot, and Tak; the southern one via Dawei and Kanchanaburi; and the middle one by way of the Three Pagoda Pass. For the first route, they proceeded by land through Kawkareik and Myawaddy on the Burmese side and arrived in Mae Sot, which was the Siamese frontier station to Tak (Halliday 1913: 7; 1917: 15)

The immigrants were welcomed by Siam. For example, the Mon expressed that "the Lord of the golden prasada, the righteous king of Ayutthaya, was the haven of the Mon race, and on every occasion saved the lives of the Mon people" (Halliday 1913: 4; Harvey 1967: 180-181). King Mongkut also considered himself as "King of Karens" (Renard 1980b: 23). Siamese kings made use of the immigrants as useful laborers and border guards (Renard 1980b: 21; Scott 2009: 272; Wyatt 2004: 113, 135-136).

In addition to warfare, millennial movements played an important role among the Karen. Devastating turmoils imbued millennial ideas that peaked in the 1820s among the Karen (Keyes 1979: 45; Stern 1968: 305-306). Hovemyr (1989) also asserts that a central motive behind Karen Christian missionary zeal into Siam was to search for the Karen king. In addition to these political and religious changes, the increase in the Karen population rendered traditional upland cultivation difficult in their areas. Therefore, they had to move down to the lowland areas, including Mae Sot.

Impact of Colonization and Nation-Building

The British Colonization of Myanmar and the Migration of People

The British engagement in Myanmar virtually ended the confrontations between the archrival kingdoms. The British become a prominent player in Mae Sot's development story. After the first Anglo-Burmese war of 1824-1826, the British took possession of Tanintharyi along with Rakhine (Arakan), Assam, and Manipur. The British massively developed Mawlamyine lying opposite the Burmese port of Mottama as a capital for the colonized areas for military and economy (Furnivall 1991 [1939]: 5-6). Under the auspices of the British, Mawlamyine experienced significant economic progress, eventually surpassing Mottama in terms of its economic importance.

British colonizers attempted to enhance overland trade by attracting Chinese merchants (Renard 1980a: 135-136). This was well recorded in the stories of Richard's missions to Siam. On several of his trips to Chiang Mai from Mawlamyine via the overland route, passing through Myawaddy and Mae Sot, he was persistent in attracting Chinese merchants in Chiang Mai to extend their trade activities to Mawlamyine (Farrington 2004). Also, the British attempted to construct railway lines linking Mawlamyine and Chiang Mai to enhance the speed of the journey (Colquhoun and Hallet 1885; Hallett 1890; Renard 1980a: 170-171). Besides, they paid particular attention to teak forests along the Moei River. Goods from Manchester and Birmingham were distributed inside Siam through the Mawlamyine-Mae Sot-Tak route (McCarthy 1994

[1900]: 2)

Given the expanded business opportunities in the trade route between Mawlamyine and inland areas, diverse groups of merchants used Mae Sot as a stopover at first and a residential place as time passed. Ethnic Chinese from various parts of Myanmar and Yunnan began to set up their residency there to gain business opportunities opened by the British colonization of lower Myanmar. Also, the other Burmese moved into the Siamese areas to pursue livelihoods. For instance, the people who cut teak in Tak were Burmese hired by the Borneo Company (Nai Banchaphusmasathan 1985). Along with these groups of people, northern Thais, as latecomers, migrated to Mae Sot, notably from Lampang. Besides, a group of Bengal Muslims and, later on, Sikhs and Hindus came to Mae Sot, passing through Myanmar (Anurak 1998).

Although the expansion of economic opportunities in lower Myanmar drew various groups of people to Mae Sot, the population size of Mae Sot remained small. Still, inconvenient environmental conditions restricted substantial population growth. Bastian's journey in 1862-1863 (Bastian 2004 [1866]; 2005 [1867]) gives some glimpses about then Mae Sot. He was on the journey to Bangkok from Myanmar, passed through Myawaddy, and crossed the Moei River, staying in Mae Sot in November 1862 before continuing his journey to Tak and Bangkok.[14] According to him,

14 The name "Mae Sot" does not appear in his story. After crossing the Moei River, he arrived in "Maiteta" which, according to Anurak (personal dialogue, December 2005), is "Mae Tao" village where a border checkpoint is located at present days. However, Bastian mentioned that he arrived there *the next day* after crossing the Burmese-Siamese border and "Maiteta" was the settlement area where the Siamese official was residing (Bastian 2005: 1-2). From that source, "Maiteta" can be assumed to be the town area of Mae Sot. He might not have had a clear understanding of geographical names.

Mae Sot was a very lonely place with Karen villages surrounding it. He saw a Chinese caravan carrying luxury goods from Myanmar to Siam. During his jungle journey from Mae Sot to Tak, Bastian encountered Siamese traders who, carrying their wares in baskets on their backs, were on their way to the border station. He later met a train of elephants that belonged to them (2005: 8-9). His accounts testify that Mae Sot was a small settlement area at the time, though various groups began settling and merchants stopovered there.

In contrast, according to his accounts (2005: 11-17), Tak was a lively and bustling town. The Chinese constituted a sizeable part of the population and mainly lived in the market quarters.[15] Tak was a rallying point for border trade with Mawlamyine and an overland entrepot where goods from Chiang Mai, Sukhothai, and Laos were gathered. Inconvenient transportation and jungle routes still prevented Mae Sot from taking over Tak as a significant overland trade station, though the importance of Mae Sot continued to grow over the years.

Migration transformed Mae Sot into a settlement place beyond a mere trading stopover. A kind of social system developed due to the immigration of various groups of people. However, newly migrating people first maintained social relationships within their own groups. In those days, the feature of a plural society where people were segregated according to racial lines (Furnivall 1944; 1956) was evident. For instance, the earlier settlers, especially the Karen, did not integrate with the new immigrants. Therefore, they moved to other marginal places when their initial settlement areas were

15 The king of Thonburi, Taksin, was once a governor of Tak. The Teochiu Chinese trading community contributed considerably to his success (Wyatt 2004: 123-124).

encroached upon by subsequent immigrants. It seems that existing Karen lifestyles, mainly based on slash-and-burn agriculture, were incompatible with the newly emerging commercial environment enhanced by commerce-driven immigration. However, a group of the earlier settlers, the Shan, solidly maintained their way of life. They began their settlement around where the District Office of Mae Sot is currently located. As Buddhists, they built their temple, Wat Mae Sot Na Dan, in 1857 (Anurak 1998: 79). Their settlement concentrated in the inner parts of Mae Sot town between the Intharakhiri Road and the Prasatwithi Road. The Chinese congregated around the Sriphanit Road, the central area of Mae Sot in the old days. Their industriousness and skillfulness in doing business led to their economic prosperity. They engaged in the brewery, goldsmith, butchery, and hotel industries (Anurak 1998: 15).

Unlike the non-Thai people, such as the Shan, the Chinese, and the Burman, who set up their residence in the central area of Mae Sot town, the northern Thai people did not necessarily venture into the inner area. They began their settlement on the outskirts of Mae Sot such as Mae Pa, Mae Ku, Mae Tao, Mae Ka Sa, and Pha Wo, with some groups settling in the central area of Mae Sot (Anurak 1998: 2, 16). The Muslims, originally from Bangladesh, established their dwellings around the Sriphanit Road near the Mae Sot Hospital after migrating from Myanmar (Anurak 1998: 20). A road named "Thanon Islambamrung" remains there, showing that they were a dominant group there. They built a mosque along that road. Their main economic field was trading.

Over time, various ethnic groups gradually molded into *chao Mae Sot* (The people of Mae Sot) beyond the pluralistic patterns that characterized initial settlement. In adapting to the local environments, each of them increasingly interacted with others in their everyday lives, although this did not lead to the total loss of individual ethnic identities. Although *chao Mae Sot* saw the increasing intervention of the central government since the later part of the nineteenth century, geographical remoteness made it conducive for them to maintain their way of life. Although the Moei river became an agreed borderline between the British and Siam in 1868 (Pitch 2007: 366), it did not restrict people across the border from developing relationships with each other (Anurak 1998: 23). The river was not a dividing boundary but a place for breeding the identity of the particular locality.

Seasonal festivals such as *songkran* and New Year's Day played a significant role in developing inter-group relationships. These festivals brought people not just from Mae Sot but also from Myawaddy together in collective celebration. Especially during *songkran* festivals, the people from each side part in cultural performances, including sports events such as swimming contests in the Moei River (Anurak 1998: 26-28). Buddhist ceremonies such as the Buddhist lent and merit-giving contributed to developing inter-ethnic mixtures among people (Anurak 1998: 25).

Interestingly, during those days, it was from Myanmar to Mae Sot that the modern cultural wave flowed. Under the auspices of the British, Myanmar tasted the modern ways of life earlier than Mae Sot. In the eyes of the people of Mae Sot, the Burmese appeared to enjoy the privileges of modern things. The style of Burmese ladies was so charming that they attracted the people of Mae Sot. Silent films from Myanmar were played in a theater-like building in Mae Sot. The people of Mae Sot learned modern lifestyles, such as drinking tea in the afternoon, eating cookies and cakes, and playing football from Myanmar. They also went to Myanmar to take pictures, which was unavailable in Mae Sot then. The rich people and the civil servants of Mae Sot often visited Myanmar to look at Myanmar's modern development (Anurak 1998: 29-30).

The Making of a National Town

While Mae Sot grew in population, the Bangkok regime attempted to stretch its influence to remote areas from the late 1890s. When British and French colonialists threatened territorial integrity and independence, Siam was desperate to reform the prevailing system of government (Tej 1977: 14). From the second half of the nineteenth century, Siam launched a series of reforms in various parts of the state, notably the provincial administration. The key to the reform of the provincial administration lay in centralization (Tej 1977: 39).

In the early reforms of the provincial administration, Siam focused on strengthening the defense of the threatened areas of the kingdom. The guard demanded administrative, judicial, and financial changes to the provinces. The Bangkok regime employed local noblemen as government officials. It also engaged in judicial autonomy and economic sectors for central control. Apart from the administrative changes, the government attempted to establish close physical contact with the entire country by posting mapping groups headed by McCarthy to all parts of Siam. There were significant improvements in communications during those days (Tej 1977: 61-75; Thongchai 1994: 119; Vandergeest and Peluso 1995: 397).

Towards the end of the nineteenth century, Bangkok effectively became an imperialist power by consolidating the previous tributary states into the direct circle of Siam, which can be called "internal territorialization" (Thongchai 1994: 145-148; Vandergeest and Peluso 1995: 397). Bangkok's intervention became prominent, with Prince Damrong heading the Ministry of the Interior in the last decade of the nineteenth under the support of King Chulalongkorn. Damrong transformed the Ministry of the North into the modern Ministry of the Interior. He made more radical and massive drives to reform the provincial administration. He came up with a new administrative system called the *thesaphiban* system. Here, several provinces were grouped into a single organizational unit (*monthon*, "circle") in a similar manner to the royal commissionerships established earlier in Chiang Mai and Phuket (Wyatt 2004: 194). In this system, Tak Province was under *monthon* Nakhonsawan, established in 1894 (Tej 1977: 101, 271). The central government also attempted to have firm control at the district, subdistrict, and village levels. Local noblemen were transformed into district officers, while below the district level, the direct masters of serfs were replaced with village heads and subdistrict chiefs (*kamnan*). The Ministry of the Interior created administrative villages and subdistricts, placing several villages clumped into a subdistrict (*tambon*). The village heads were instructed to elect among themselves a *kamnan* (Tej 1977: 111; Vandergeest and Peluso 1995: 399).

Reflecting on the above occurrences, Mae Sot saw the interventions of Bangkok and the subsequent administrative developments at that time. Initially, the Karen were assigned to be in charge of border control in the first half of the nineteenth century. In 1845 Bangkok extended its rule beyond Mae Sot to Tha Song Yang, the northernmost district of Tak Province (Renard 1980b: 21).[16]

The administrative change of Mae Sot started with rearranging the guard post. During the reign of Rama V, the border post (*dan* Mae Lamao) located in Mae Lamao village moved to adjacent places of Mae Sot near the Moei River with the expansion to four posts: *dan* Intharakhiri, *dan* Chai, *dan* Phon, and *dan* Chiangthong. While the first border post was in Mae Ramat district north of Mae Sot, the others were located inside the district area of Mae Sot. Administratively, all of them were initially under Muang Tak of *monthon* Nakhon Sawan. However, in 1898, they were dissolved, incorporated into a newly created *amphoe* Mae Sot, and separated from the previous administrative position. Moreover, *phra* Intharakhiri,[17] who had been in charge of *dan* Mae Ramat and was Karen, became the first *nay amphoe* (Head of District) of Mae Sot (Anurak 1998: 83).

16 Before that, Chiang Mai had governed Tha Song Yang. Mae Hong Son province had initially included Tha Song Yang. However, when boundaries were redrawn, the district was shifted to Tak Province (Renard 1980b: 27). Even Tak, throughout its history, had changed allegiance on several occasions from Sukhothai to Chiang Mai and Ayutthaya at the end of the eighteenth century (Renard 1980a: 114).

17 The name Intharakhiri traces back to 1661 when the Siamese forces in the reign of King Narai invaded northern Thailand. The forces captured many principalities of Karen and Lawa under the suzerainty of Chiang Mai, including Muang Intharakhiri (Damrong 2001: 222). Intharakhiri is Mae Ramat today where one of the guard posts was located as mentioned above. Renard mentioned that the Karen were in charge of Intharakhiri throughout history. The title of the chief person was awarded and passed down in recognition of the place of authority. Therefore, there were a lot of *phra* Intharakhiri in history. However, most of them were considered Karen (Renard 1980a: 57). Anurak mentions that the first *nay amphoe*, *phra* Intharakhiri, was also Karen (personal communication).

The state implemented several modern projects in Mae Sot. In 1881 the telegraph line was connected from Tak to Mawlamyine, passing through Mae Sot and Myawaddy (Anurak 1998: 3; Thongchai 1994: 118). Mapping and topographical surveys occurred to draw boundaries between Siam and British Myanmar and between provinces. During 1882-1883, a map of the boundary between Tak and Chiang Mai came out to settle their dispute over the woodcutting tax (Thongchai 1994: 118). During 1890-1891, a mapping of the boundary on the frontier between Siam and Myanmar was conducted (Thongchai 1994: 124). In 1896, a team of Anglo-Thai boundary expedition marched to Mae Sot after investigations in the Three Pagoda Pass and Umphang areas (Renard 1980a: 191). Mae Sot seemed to gradually become a part of the "geo-body" through Siam's attempts at the turn of the century.

Throughout the earlier part of the twentieth century, Mae Sot was on its way to becoming a full-fledged administrative district, equipped with a series of state-related organizations: the first public school in 1915; the police station in 1920; the border checkpoint in 1927; the prison in 1938; the *thesaban* (municipal office) in 1939; the customs office 1940; the border patrol police in 1954; and the Mae Sot Hospital in 1958 (Anurak 1998).

Also, the infrastructure of transportation developed: the Mae Sot airport, built after the First World War, commenced passenger service in 1932 though it was interrupted during the Second World War;[18] and in 1954, the condition of the Mae Sot-Tak road improved to accommodate vehicles though it was one-lane without pavement

18 During the Second World War, Japanese armies marched to Myanmar through Mae Sot (Anurak 1998: 33).

(Anurak 1998).

During the 1960s, Mae Sot saw ongoing development. Road conditions between Mae Sot and Tak further improved. After Prime Minister Thanom Kittikachorn visited Mae Sot along that route, he realized the importance of the road to connect with Myanmar. He sought financial aid from the Australian government during his visit to Australia. In 1970, with Australia's technological and financial assistance, the road was made convenient and safe, though it is still a one-lane path (Anurak 1998: 12-13).

It is vital in developing a national identity among the people of Mae Sot to witness the physical presence of the monarch. In 1964, King Bhumibol Adulyadej and the Queen visited Mae Sot for the first time. They made another visit to Mae Sot in 1978. Afterward, the palace initiated several projects, such as those on agriculture (Anurak 1998). The actual appearance of the monarch, even in the remote town of Mae Sot, might have precipitated the town into a "national" town by imbuing the core idea of Thai nationalism in the minds of the people of Mae Sot.

Throughout the period, the government generally attempted to enhance its ability in the affairs of remote areas. In the long run, it wanted to increase the integration of remote villages into the national economy (Wyatt 2004: 286).

The penetration of Bangkok and Mae Sot's subsequent incorporation into the state administrative system did not necessarily occur without local resistance and discrepancies between state aspiration and actual implementation. For example, a retired governor of Tak encouraged the provincial officials to resist the new governor sent from outside the province, according to Prince

Damrong's report to King Rama V in 1899 (Tej 1977: 174). Mae Sot district officials posted by the central government from the outside could not correctly communicate with the local people because their languages were not mutually understandable. The officials spoke central Thai, while people in Mae Sot spoke northern Thai, primarily mixed with other ethnic languages. Therefore, they had to hire interpreters when approaching the locals. Demographically speaking, the portion of central Thais in Mae Sot's population was exclusively small, and the central Thai style was not a model for people in Mae Sot. Northern Thai or Lanna lifestyles were becoming an integrating force for various groups in Mae Sot without the total loss of the elements of each ethnic group.

Given that situation, introducing the central elements through official channels was very alien to the people of Mae Sot and at times encountered resistance from them. Besides, Mae Sot and its adjacent mountains kept offering sanctuaries for not just Burmese ethnic minorities but also members of the Communist Party of Thailand (Race 1974). The central government's endeavors in placing the border town under firm control were never fruitful though not stoppable.

Although Mae Sot continued to be influenced by the center as time went by, its influence was relatively minimal in comparison with the impact of the political development of Myanmar on the fashioning of Mae Sot. In other words, the town was more susceptible and indebted to the other side of the border, particularly in economic development.

Black Markets and a New Wave of Migration: From 1962 to1988

The Burmese Way to Socialism and the Flourishing Black Markets

Burmese democracy, full of detrimental disputes and the mutinies of communists and ethnic insurgent groups from her independence, collapsed in 1962, allowing the military to seize power through a coup.[19] Subsequently, the military government projected "the Burmese Way to Socialism," which drove Myanmar to be hermetic and self-isolating. Private sectors and properties were nationalized and confiscated. The country's doors were closed to its neighboring countries and the rest of the world.

A turning point also arose in ethnic politics. The Karen National Union, which had engaged in the late 1940s, lost its territorial occupation in the adjacent areas of Yangon, Toungoo, and Delta region towards 1960 and consequently moved its military bases to the eastern border areas of Myanmar, nearby areas of Mae Sot (Lintner 1999: 297). However, it soon rehabilitated its military and administrative capacities and maintained a firm control in those areas, running a *de facto* nation-state.

The closed-door policy of the military regime resulted in a scarcity of consumer goods in the country. The situation led to the engendering of the black markets in the borderland, especially in the adjacent areas near Mae Sot. From 1963, the black markets saw a dramatic development, though, in the early 1950s, customs gates had

19 For details, see Taylor (1987) and Smith (1999a).

been opened at several KNU posts along the border. The first new Karen customs gate was opened at Phalu, south of Myawaddy, in the sixth brigade area in 1964. The following year Bo Mya[20] opened another gate at Wangkha in his 7th brigade area to the north (Smith 1999a: 283).

Martin Smith (1999a: 283) documents the proliferation of the black markets as follows,

> By the 1970s Bo Mya's main base at Kawmoorah was sometimes producing as much as one *lakh* kyat[21] in a single day's trading when up to 1,000 cattle would splash across the Moei River into Thailand at the end of the long journey across the Dawna Range from central Burma. Transported in the other direction were radios, watches, high-quality sarongs and other manufactured goods now unavailable in Burma. Added to this income was revenue from timber mills and tin and antimony mines run jointly with local Thai businessmen. Vast profits were generated though opium, which was an important source of income for insurgent groups in the Shan State, has always been strictly prohibited. In the peak year of 1983 KNU Finance Minister, Pu Ler Wah, estimated incomes at 500 million kyat (£50m at the official exchange rate), an astonishing figure for an otherwise impoverished backwater.

The above observation concurred with local informants involved in the operation of the black markets. Cattle were voluminously transported from the Burmese side, while consumer goods and

20 He passed away at 79 on December 24, 2006 in Mae Sot. See the reports of Bangkok Post (2006) and Irrawaddy (2006f; 2006g) on his death.

21 The kyat is the currency of Myanmar. 1 USD was equivalent to around 1,000 kyat in the early 2010s, but by the end of 2022, it was about 2,100 kyat.

machinery, such as sewing machines, came from the Thai side.[22] Jewelry made up a significant portion of that trade too. Gold was often a means of payment for Burmese buyers. Jade and ruby attracted even overseas merchants, mainly from Hong Kong. Merchants from Hong Kong used to visit and stay in Mae Sot to acquire jade from the Burmese traders. According to Chang (2003; 2004), Yunnanese merchants were very active in this jade trade, and Mae Sot took over from Mae Sai as a central trading place for jade by the 1980s.

The black markets' impact on Myanmar's national economy during those days was enormous. Though exact figures were not attainable, estimates of the illegal trade vary from between 50 to 85 percent of the total official trade in the mid-1980s (Myat Thein 2004: 80). According to Khin (1988: 94), about two-thirds of goods in the black markets were smuggled in from Thailand. The total illegal trade was thought to have a turnover of up to 50 percent of official trading.

The effect of the black markets on Mae Sot was dramatic and tremendous. The sleepy outpost of Mae Sot rapidly turned into a bustling new market town and the pivotal center of much of this new trade (Smith 1999a: 283). The large black market operations induced another migration phase comprising business people from Bangkok who were primarily Chinese but occasionally included some Indian Sikhs. New immigrants had relatively more capital and resources than the people of Mae Sot. They soon dominated the town's central area and transformed its landscapes into a highly commercialized

22 For details of items traded between Thailand and Myanmar in the black markets, see Mya Than (1992: 57-58).

place by establishing their shops and welcoming new customers. Although they had business relationships with Bangkok, their hectic business dealings forced them to stay in Mae Sot permanently.

Moreover, the relatively inconvenient transportation system discouraged them from retaining their close relationships with Bangkok. In the beginning, male migration was the main pattern. However, entire families followed them to Mae Sot, hoping that family labor could be used in their expanded business fields, keeping families close to their new settlements. Throughout 1962-1988, this group of new domestic migrants became crucial figures in the town's economy and the main components of the Tak Chamber of Commerce, the head office based in Mae Sot, not in the provincial town. Their identities transformed from migrants to settlers as time passed.

The lives of the people of Mae Sot were intimately related to the operation of the black markets. The number of people involved in the trade was vast; for instance, my informants said more than a thousand porters engaged in transportation from Mae Sot to Wangkha. Many shopkeepers expanded their businesses in connection with Bangkok, from which goods were delivered to Mae Sot before entering the black markets. Traditional commercial relationships with northern Thailand were replaced by connections with Bangkok as the capital city experienced rapid industrialization and subsequently provided the necessary goods for the black markets.

The black markets equally attracted the massive participation of the Burmese. Besides merchants, many Burmese porters transported goods from the black markets to the inner places of Myanmar. On their journey, they passed through jungle routes protected by the KNU soldiers up to Mawlamyine and then took the train to Yangon. The open black market, popularly known as St John's Shopping Center, operated to meet people's need for consumer goods in Yangon (Aung Kin 1983, cited in Myat Thein 2004: 81). In this commodity moving chain, an incredible number of Burmese, as well as Thais, were involved. Mae Sot became the central position in the circulation of black market goods.

Although many Burmese people flowed into Mae Sot, they, unlike domestic migrants from Bangkok shown above, did not necessarily pursue permanent residence in Mae Sot since the Burmese sides, including the black market areas, provided substantial economic opportunities. However, they kept flowing in and out of the town in intimate social and economic relations with it. The fortune the Burmese acquired in running food stalls in Wangkha and Phalu and transporting goods between Wangkha and Mawlamyine did not compel them to pursue imminent livelihood pursuits inside Mae Sot.

Nevertheless, massive cross-border movements of people molded a strong sense of collective identity as borderlanders regardless of nationality. Still, in the condition that the penetrations of the two neighboring states were still limited, people in the borderland enjoyed relative autonomy under the auspice of the para-state organization, notably the KNU. The borderland remained a non-state space where unofficial movements of people and goods prevailed, and the dividing of nationalities lost legitimacy.

The KNU and Mae Sot

The prolific development of the black markets strengthened the capacity of the KNU. Although the military bases became confined to the borderland, the profit generated by tax (roughly seven percent) on trade enabled the KNU to possess weaponry. Significantly, it increased the political clout of Bo Mya, who was in charge of the areas in the black markets. Based on successful economic and military operations, he eventually became president of the KNU in 1976 (Smith 1999a: 284-285).

In general, the relationships between Mae Sot and the KNU were friendly. However, there was a woeful exception. On May 15, 1960, a military band of the KNU inflicted horrible damage on Mae Sot. The group burnt down the District Office of Mae Sot, previously located in the current location of the Mae Sot police station, and destroyed communication systems. The people of Mae Sot and district officials fled to Mae Pa village. Shortly, the band retreated to the Burmese side. This incident became a national issue, and then Prime Minister Sarit and government officials visited Mae Sot to examine what happened and increase security alerts. The reasons behind this incident were not disclosed in Anurak's book (1998: 33-34). However, according to Bo Mya in his biography (n.d.: 83-88), Thai merchants deceived the leaders of the military band. The Karen group delivered 300 heads of cattle to the Thai merchants, who promised to pay for them soon. However, the merchants never turned up, which provoked the Karen band to retaliate. Bo Mya, who was a branch leader in the seventh brigade at that time, came over to Mae Sot to settle the case with Thai authorities. He assured them that the KNU would never cause trouble in the future. This meeting portrayed Bo Mya as a diplomatic figure to the Thai authorities.

Despite such an awful incident, the KNU and the Thai authorities maintained amicable relationships throughout the years. It was mainly because of the KNU's security roles at the border. Under Bo Mya's staunchly nationalist leadership, the KNU undoubtedly gave the Thai government crucial help in blocking the spread of communist insurgency in the region and frustrated the Communist Party of Thailand (CPT)'s attempts to link up with the Communist Party of Burma (CPB). Without the solid presence of the KNU in "liberated areas" along the border, the CPB in Dawei-Myeik (Mergui) would have been able to forge a link with the CPT in the forests of Mae Sariang and Umphang, and the connection would have been further extended to the communist parties of China and Malaysia. The KNU's assistance was not confined to the Kawthoolei[23] side of the border. Thai officers requested it to cross into Thailand to disarm Karen villagers who had been organized by the CPT (Smith 1999a: 299).

The cordial relationships were reflected in Bo Mya's statement, where the KNU was likened to a "Foreign Legion" for Thailand, guarding their borders and preventing links between the Burmese communists and the Thai communists (Smith 1999a: 299). In return for the KNU's positive role in support of Thailand, the Thai authorities allowed them to stay on Thai soil and buy arms, ammunition, and other supplies in Thailand. Also, the Thais attached special agents who served as observers and advisers to the Karen units (Lintner 1999: 299). Given this background, the families of KNU leaders began settling in Mae Sot in addition to their residence in the liberated zones of the border. For example, the sixth brigade

23 It is the Karen name for the state that the KNU was trying to establish. It roughly covers Karen State that the Burmese government designated. Kawthoolei means "the land without evil."

commander of the KNU, Shwe Hser and his family members sometimes came and stayed in their house in Mae Sot.[24] The Thai authorities also issued travel permits and provided amenities for rebel leaders who wanted to go to Chiang Mai or Bangkok under the auspices of Thai intelligence agencies. Often the journeys were rallied from Mae Sot.

The people in Mae Sot also benefited from the presence of the KNU since it protected the black markets where the economic activities of Mae Sot were intimately tied. Without security services in the borderland provided by the KNU, border trade would not have prospered, and it would have restricted the economic welfare of ordinary people in Mae Sot.

Massive Migration and Migrant Institutions: From 1988

Political Crisis in Myanmar and Its Impact

The Thailand-Myanmar borderland saw significant geopolitical and geo-economical changes in the late 1980s, profoundly impacting Mae Sot. The military regime drove the economy of Myanmar into an abysmal situation. The export volume decreased to 2 percent of GDP in 1987/1988 from 16 percent in 1961/1962. The country was almost bankrupt as the external public debt rolled into massive amounts; the debt/GDP increased from 20 to 40 percent in 1986 when debt-service obligations equaled 58.24 percent of

24 I met his descendants in Mae Sot.

export earnings. Myanmar was on the brink of bankruptcy. The situation compelled the government to seek "Least Developed Country (LDC)"[25] status in the United Nations in 1987 to reduce interest rates and receive new financial grants from international organizations like the IMF (Mya Thein 2004: 77-80). The Burmese Way to Socialism, an idiosyncratic mixture of Marxist, Buddhist, and nationalist ideology, eventually led Myanmar, once considered among the potential in Asia, to one of the world's ten poorest nations (Smith 1999a: 24).

Burmese citizens suffered from harsh conditions. They had to go through a shortage of essential everyday goods and financial insecurity caused by the government's chronic demonetization practices in attempts to normalize the black market economy. People ceased to contain their tolerance against the regime. Outrageous anti-government demonstrations took place in March 1988 and soon spread to the country. People in every sector, including students, workers, monks, farmers, teachers, and government employers, participated in the uprisings. In response to this situation, the government put down the demonstrations by using force on one hand. At the same time, it tried to introduce a multi-party political system with the abdication of Ne Win, who had been the head of the government, and with the introduction of a civilian leader, Dr. Maung Maung, on the other hand. However, this *ad hoc* democratization never calmed people's disgruntlement against the government.

25 LDC status has some requirements: the per capita income should be below US$200, the industry should be less than 10 percent of GNP, and literacy is less than 20 percent. Myanmar was said to have adjusted its estimate of literacy downwards to qualify for that status (Myat Thein 2004: 84).

The political crisis ultimately led to the introduction of a refashioned military regime in the name of the State Law and Order Restoration Council (SLORC)[26] through a coup on September 18, 1988. The new military regime attempted to bring the country back to a normal state by suppressing democratic uprisings. In doing so, an uncountable number of people lost their lives. Those who could not bear the dreadful conditions marched towards the border to take refuge. Thousands of students and political activists boarded cars and buses bound for Mawlamyine and Kawkareik and, from there, trekking through the jungles and over the hills to the Thai border near Mae Sot. Others went to the nearby Three Pagoda Pass or headed for Victoria Point in the far southeast (Lintner 1999: 353). This exodus took similar routes to the fugitives or refugees in the pre-modern period, as shown earlier. It was a recurring event.

Meanwhile, the new junta officially discarded the defunct closed-door economic policy and began promoting open-door policies, mainly to neighboring countries. It attempted to formalize trading and political relations with them by nullifying the operations of the black markets. In this regard, the government needed to firmly control the borderland where natural resources were abundant to develop the formal and official economic relationships with the bordering countries. However, ethnic insurgent groups prevailed. Thus, it sought cease-fire agreements with many ethnic militant groups, such as the United Wa State Party and the Shan State Army (Smith 1999b: 50), while operating strenuous and massive military expeditions towards non-ceasefire groups, notably the KNU.

26 The SLORC was officially dissolved and replaced with the State Peace and Development Council (SPDC) in November 1997 (Lang 2002: 8).

Alongside military operations, the notorious "Four Cuts" campaign[27] devastated the border areas by the late 1980s (Smith 1999a: 397). Consequently, the campaign pushed many people to the other side of the border while others remained internally displaced.

The Development of the Borderland and Wave of Economic Migrants and Refugees

While Myanmar suffered a woeful economic decline and social devastation towards the late 1980s, Thailand was on the track of rapid economic growth: the country boasted 9.5 percent growth in 1987 and 13.2 percent in 1988. With this development, Thailand underwent a rapid change in economic formation. The proportion of agriculture in GDP decreased, yet the industrial sector's share expanded with the need for trade and markets (Buszynski 1994: 723). Regarding the geopolitical situation, Thailand was released from its obsession with national security as the Indochina conflicts ended with the CPT's demise. Thus, Thailand's foreign policy needed adjustments to reflect the region's changing economic and political situations.

Given the situation, Thailand's border areas no longer served as buffer zones; instead, in the new political and economic context of regional relations, they served as gateways for trade and investment (Battersby 1998/1999: 487). Thailand aspired to turn "battlefields into trading markets" and developed economic ties with neighboring

27 The strategy was officially endorsed in 1968 and was known as *pya ley pay* in Burmese. Fundamentally, the campaign aimed to cut the insurgents off from their support system which included food supplies, funding, intelligence and recruits (Lang 2002: 38). It was substantially introduced in the mid-80s in southeast Myanmar (Smith 1999a: 397)

countries, particularly Myanmar, becoming a focal point (Grundy-Warr *et al.* 1997: 99).

General Chavalit Yongchaiyudh's visit to Myanmar in 1988 symbolically heralded a new era in relations between Bangkok and Yangon. He and a hundred of his delegates were the first foreign diplomatic group to give recognition to the newly formed military regime. Among the projects discussed were an increase in the official trade in teak and, to the alarm of Karen villagers, the construction of hydroelectric dams along the Moei and Salween rivers in the heart of Kawthoolei to provide electricity to both countries. Besides, by early 1989, twenty concession areas had been granted along the Thailand-Myanmar border, and 16,000 tons of teak logs and 500,000 tons of other hardwood logs were contracted to enter Thailand. Thai fishery companies also acquired permission to catch 250,000 tons of fish in Burmese waters (Battersby 1998/1999: 477; Hirsh 1995: 244; Lintner 1999: 357-358; Smith 1999a: 397).

The roles of ethnic insurgent groups, notably the KNU, which had acted as border guards against the threat of communists, lost their relevance in Thailand's new geopolitical and geo-economical strategy. The Thai government sought to have more formalized relationships with the Burmese government at the expense of the insurgent groups. In the eyes of the Thai government, having formal economic relations with the Burmese government would bring much more profit and thus be rational. It led to a "constructive engagement" policy where economic reasons come before anything else in engagements with Myanmar (Grundy-Warr *et al.* 1997: 98-99).

As Myanmar and Thailand began to formalize their political and economic relations and the Burmese troops increasingly encroached on the borderland, the black markets that had massively operated near Mae Sot unavoidably faced a steep decline by the late 1980s. In 1988 the KNU's income plummeted by sixty percent (Smith 1999a: 396). As the Burmese government developed Myawaddy as the official trading outpost in the 1ate 1980s, Thai business people began to send their export goods through Myawaddy posts, not through the black markets. By 1992, the black markets in Wangkha and Phalu were eventually out of date.

However, the disappearance of the black markets, which had significantly impacted the economic development of Mae Sot, never caused a decline in the economic importance of Mae Sot. Many Burmese who had suffered the social and economic devastation in Myanmar now flew into the town in pursuit of economic opportunities. Also, those whose livelihoods had previously relied on the black markets advanced to Mae Sot to find economic opportunities. Mae Sot accommodated the unprecedented size of "economic migrants" from 1988 onwards. In contrast to the relatively gradual population increase in the previous periods, this new wave of migration took place abruptly, and the number of migrants soon outnumbered that of the Thai locals.

As there was cheap labor available in Mae Sot, factories began to relocate in Mae Sot. The relocation of factories was backed by the decentralization policies of the Thai government in its attempts to rectify the extreme economic disparity between Bangkok and the peripheral areas of the country. In those policies, Mae Sot received special attention from the government due to its good location. Moreover, in the broader regional perspective, the roles of Mae Sot were regarded as incredibly important in promoting regional cooperation through programs such as the Greater Mekong Subregion (GMS) program[28] (ADB 2001; Maneepong 2002/2003; 2004; 2005). Under the GMS program, the Asian Development Bank (ADB) also devised the project of the East-West Corridor,[29] which supported various infrastructure projects in Mae Sot, acknowledging Mae Sot's role as part of a strategic network (Maneepong 2005: 266). The projects included the construction of the Thai-Myanmar Friendship Bridge in 1997, which connects Mae Sot and Myawaddy across the Moei River; the road between Mae Sot and Tak, a section of the Asian Highways, was improved and expanded. To exploit expanded business opportunities, more and more factories entered Mae Sot. The number of factories increased from 118 in 1993 to 218 in 2000 (Maneepong 2002/2003: 91). Garment factories constituted dominant figures in employment and investment (Maneepong 2005: 280-281). These factories opened in cooperation with overseas partners, notably from Hong Kong and Taiwan (BLSO 2002; Maneepong 2005: 282). The developments eventually led Mae Sot to surpass Tak's provincial district as the province's economic center.

The economic expansion of Mae Sot pulled more migrants throughout the 1990s. It became a prevailing scene for most shops to hire illegal or undocumented Burmese workers. Others worked as *mae ban*, domestic workers. Though the government introduced the registration scheme in the late 1990s, it was only effective in

28 It was formed in 1992 under the agreement of six countries, including China, Myanmar, Thailand, Laos, Cambodia, and Vietnam.

29 The Economic Corridor approach was first discussed in late 1998 as a necessary means of developing further cooperation of the GMS. The East-West Economic Corridor stretches across four GMS countries from Moulmein in Buma, through Mae Sot in Thailand and Laos, to Da Nang in Vietnam (ADB 2001: xi).

factories. Other sectors, such as shops and the domestic arena, still engaged in plenty of illegal employment.

In tandem with economic migrants, Mae Sot faced the flow of refugees. As the Burmese government kept consolidating the border areas, people in those areas fled to the other side of the border to enter refugee camps near Mae Sot. Most dramatically, the KNU lost Manerplaw in 1995, which had served as a head-quarter for a long time, due to the split with the Democratic Karen Buddhist Army (DKBA)[30] and its cooperation with the Burmese government in subjugating the KNU (Lintner 1995; 1999: 413-414). Consequently, ethnic insurgent groups such as the KNU and other National Democratic Front (NDF)[31] member groups searched for refuge in Mae Sot and restructured their military strategy to guerilla warfare. Also, Burmese political organizations such as the National League for Democracy (NLD) and the All Burma Students' Democratic Front (ABSDF) sought sanctuary in the town.

Furthermore, sub-KNU organizations, including the Karen Youth Organization (KYO) and the Karen Women's Organization (KWO), came over to Mae Sot and began to be involved in activities for Karen refugees. In the series of these incidents, the number of refugees grew. When the first sizeable influx of refugees took place, their number was 10,000 in the middle of the 1980s. However, it increased rapidly to 55,000 in 1993, 80,000 in 1994, 115,000 in

30 The DKBA was said to be formed by Buddhist Karen soldiers disillusioned with their lack of influence within the Christian-dominated KNU leadership. It was also said that this split was instigated by the Burmese government. Soon after the split, the DKBA allied itself with the Burmese government (Smith: 1999a: 446-450; Lintner 1999: 413-414).

31 It was organized as an umbrella organization for ethnic insurgent groups in 1976 under the leadership of the KNU (Smith 1999a: 280).

1997, and 143,000 in 2005 (Bowles 1998; TBBC 2005).

The refugee crisis drew the attention of humanitarian relief agencies. The dominant presence of refugees in the adjacent areas of Mae Sot led them to open branch offices in the town to deliver assistance to the needy conveniently. During the 1990s, dozens of INGOs began to run their branches in Mae Sot. Eventually, in 1998, the United Nations High Commissioner for Refugees (UNHCR) also opened its regional branch in Mae Sot and commenced its activities.

Now, Mae Sot seemed to become a town with a preponderant presence of aliens while accommodating the migration of Thai business people and factory owners from inland areas such as Bangkok. Paradoxically, as the Thai government sponsored Mae Sot with various developmental projects for state purposes, the town became increasingly reliant on unauthorized people in almost every sector. Despite the government's attempts to legalize or officialize their status, for instance, by introducing the Work Permit scheme, its endeavors were never successful. Instead, we witnessed the establishment of non-state institutions by migrants in the form of migrant schools and a migrant clinic. Since establishing a Burmese migrant school in 1991 in Mae Sot, the number of migrant schools and students has massively increased. In 2010, sixty-one migrant schools accommodated over 11,000 students (Migrant Educational Co-ordination Center 2010). As of the early 2020s, the schools continued to provide education in a similar capacity. Likewise, a migrant health clinic called Cynthia Clinic provided healthcare services to hundreds of people daily. Both the migrant schools and the clinic show how the town is deeply embedded with "otherness" and, in the same vein, how others massively mark their presence even in the absence of proper legal status.

With the preponderant presence of the migrant people, the social system of the town became much more expanded, accelerating people's movement across the border. Thousands of people made border crossings daily to pursue economic, medical, and other practical opportunities. Moreover, their movement does not remain only in the borderland; once they find more fortune in other places, notably Bangkok, they embark on another journey from there. Equally, another movement from Myanmar fills the gap. This dynamic population circulation, indeed, is inherent in the border society as previous movement of moving people including fugitives, refugees, and merchants constituted the border society for years.

Conclusion: Siam Mapped?

This study has dealt with Mae Sot's history from as early as the thirteenth century. From the beginning, Mae Sot has been connected to the outside world through commerce. In particular, it has linked up between the Indian Ocean and inland areas of mainland Southeast Asia. The pre-modern kingdoms of Myanmar and Thailand used this connection for economic and military purposes. In the perennial conflicts between the two kingdoms, fugitives and refugees took sanctuary in and around Mae Sot. These pre-modern moving people laid the foundation of Mae Sot's future development as a central settlement area on the Thailand-Myanmar borderland.

Not long after the war-affected refugees migrated to the town, another wave of people, headed by merchants, flew into the town as the British began to rule lower Myanmar and were keenly interested in trade between their colony and China, passing through the Thailand-Myanmar border. The town's ethnoscape became diverse with the settlement of the Shan, the Chinese, the Muslims, and northern Thais on top of the early Karen settlers.

As Siam became a modern state at the turn of the 19th century to the 20th century, Mae Sot was nominally incorporated into the state bureaucracy system. However, given the state's geographical remoteness and limited capability, Mae Sot was predominantly a non-state space where people maintained a relatively autonomous way of life in a close connection with the other side of the border. People's geographical scale was different from the state's one. The state's project of building geo-body remained effective only on the map and was thus alien to the everyday practices of cross-border movement of people (cf. Thongchai 1994).

The prolific operation of the black markets accelerated the fluid movement of people and consequently developed Mae Sot as a central place along the Thailand-Myanmar border, leapfrogging even the provincial town. In the condition that still the two states' capability to place it under their control was limited, a non-state group, the KNU, played a significant role in facilitating the cross-border movement of goods and people.

Building upon this foundation, the borderland underwent another development phase in the dynamics of new regional politics opened by the end of the Cold War. Now, the two states consolidated their grip on each section of the borderland by physical force or development projects. At this stage, an unprecedented wave of people flooded into the other side of the border from Myanmar.

Unlike the state's intention, this movement continued to take place unauthorizedly. Although this type of movement appears to be illicit and illegitimate in the eyes of the state, it is licit and legitimate in the eyes of the borderlanders and the inherent nature of constituting the societal formation in the borderland.

Throughout history, it was the moving people, including merchants, fugitives, refugees, and migrant workers, that transformed the land into a settlement area. The town's history is deeply associated with this fluid movement of people. This continuing movement is built into the fabric of society. This deep historicity associated with the geographical formation of the borderland transcends the state's attempts to regulate the movement.

Chapter 3

Migrant Enclaves: Ghettos or Transnational Social Spaces?

Introduction

This chapter examines Burmese migrant enclaves in Mae Sot in conjunction with governance, mobility, and connectivity. As mentioned in the previous chapter, since the late 1980s, when Myanmar suffered difficult economic and political conditions, the town has been a significant destination for Burmese migrants crossing the border to seek economic opportunities and political sanctuary. Eventually, migrants far outnumbered the Thai nationals: as of 2016, the migrant population was estimated to be 200,000 compared to 100,000 Thai. The majority of Burmese migrants, however, do not possess the proper legal documents, that is, work permits. Such massive migration and settlement also dramatically transformed the town's landscape. One can easily recognize migrant enclaves scattered across the town, providing unique and contrasting patches within the urban space. Two extremes coexist: areas where the Thai, particularly the rich live are tidy and clean with modern houses; Burmese migrant enclaves, however, consist of makeshift houses, poor water supply, inadequate sanitary conditions, garbage, and dirt, while the children wear shabby clothes: seemingly they are no more than ghettos. Indeed, the local Thai often call migrant enclaves *salam*, an adopted term of the English word "slum," or *chum chon ae at* (crowded community), still carrying the negative meaning.

These "miserable" conditions are widely known and form the main component of academic works and NGO reports dealing with migrant lifestyles (e.g., IOM 2016; Saltsman 2015; Thornton 2006). In these accounts, migrants are often described as social outcasts whom both their home and host countries have abandoned. They are segregated into their residential enclaves, not mixing with the Thai population, similar to the secluded lives of the Burakumin in Japan and the Jews in medieval Europe. According to Saltsman (2015: 3), residential enclaves are "invisible slums" or "Third World" spaces. This perspective is greatly influenced by humanitarianism, which tends to regard migrant enclaves as deviant and pathological and migrants as voiceless victims who cannot escape from such deplorable ghettos. A dark cloud hangs over migrant enclaves: "Ghettos! Can anything good come from there?"[32] is the stereotypical question.

I acknowledge that these conventional approaches have raised public awareness of the plight of migrants and instigated welfare programs. It has become the norm to share the migrants' burden and to offer support in this age of global governance. However, a deeper understanding of migrants' lives and the spatial configuration of their enclaves is lost. The preoccupation with migrants suffering deplorable conditions prevents an approach dealing with them as human agents to overcome the hardship and rebuild their lives, even in precarious situations. I argue that migrants' lives are undoubtedly dynamic, intersecting illegal and legal domains, crossing international borders, and appropriating transnational connections. In this chapter, the emphasis lies on the spatial rescaling of migrant enclaves as transnational social fields beyond the conventional view of them as segregated ghettos.

32 This phrase is adapted from John 1:46 in the Bible: "Nazareth! Can anything good come from there?"

From Ghettos to Transnational Conjunctural Spaces

A ghetto is "a set of neighborhoods that are exclusively inhabited by members of one group, within which virtually all members of that group live" (Massey and Denton 1993: 18-19). An assumption is that it originates from the Hebrew "ghet," which means reclusion (Stehle 2006: 51). Indeed, the word ghetto can be traced back to medieval Europe, where it initially referred to the forced confinement of the Jews to special districts by the city's political and religious authorities. The Jews were allocated their own residential areas in which they administered their affairs according to their customs. Although not forced to reside in those areas at first, following the upheavals caused by the Crusades between the thirteenth and sixteenth centuries, the Jews were compulsorily segregated into certain places. In 1516, the city authority of Venice ordered all Jews to move into the "Ghetto Nuovo," an abandoned foundry on a remote island surrounded by high walls; they also had to wear distinctive garments and were kept under close observation by watchmen. After that, this Venetian model of the ghetto spread throughout Europe and around the Mediterranean Rim (Sennett 1994; Wacquant 2011: 6). More recently, one of the most common uses of this method was the forced ghettoization of European Jews during the Nazi regime (Stehle 2006: 51).

The term ghet began to be used in the city slums, in particular, residential areas of the East European Jews and other minority groups in the USA (Ward 1989: 2). It became widely used, especially at the outbreak of World War I when African Americans from the South were recruited en masse to northern cities (Wacquant

2011: 7-8). Alongside African Americans, during the early part of the twentieth century, Mexicans also migrated into industrial cities, notably Chicago, and voluntarily and involuntarily established segregated residential settlements. African Americans, Mexican Americans, and Whites lived in separate settlements within Chicago, and this pattern of migration and settlement persisted across the city throughout the twentieth century (De Genova 2005: 113-122).

These European and American experiences were not exceptional, leading to a seminal notion of "plural society" in colonial Southeast Asia, notably Burma and Indonesia. Coined by Furnivall (1944: 446), the term plural society means "a society comprising two or more elements or social orders which live side by side, yet without mingling, in one political unit." As discussed in the Introduction chapter, people in this society are divided into racial groups, each keeping its custom and only meeting in the marketplace (Furnivall 1956: 304). As in the USA, the critical factor behind a plural society was the migration of ethnic groups, notably the Chinese and Indians, into the colonies for economic development. Each migrant group established a segregated residential enclave, and economic occupations were distinct along ethnic lines. Furnivall regarded plural societies as pathological and something to be eventually dismantled as they developed into mature societies that would share a common social goal and promote the welfare of the society as a whole.

This pathological approach toward residential enclaves has been prevalent in other countries, notably the USA, where poverty problems were closely associated with residential conditions (Ward 1989). Earlier scholars in the USA—those of the Chicago School—particularly during the 1920s and 1930s, shared Furnivall's viewpoint (e.g., Park 1926; Wirth 1928): they regarded migrant enclaves as a natural stage in the process leading ultimately to the assimilation of the migrants. The central idea of this theory is a direct association between the degree of assimilation and the spatial pattern of dispersal. Thus, the proportion of residential segregation was equated to the levels of migrant assimilation into the wider society: a high level of segregation was identified as non-assimilation, while a low level reflected greater assimilation (Peach 2003: 99-100). In other words, social interaction, the key to assimilation, was controlled by geographical proximity and inter-group socializing.

However, migrant enclaves did not disappear but persisted, proving the failure of the Chicago School's evolutionary approach, which did not consider that human residential spaces reflect power (Lefebvre 1991). The ghettos were developed by state policies of public housing and urban planning that encouraged the spatial and social separation of the minority from the majority (Wacquant 2011: 9-10). Scholars now point out that the urban ghettos must be understood in terms of the structure and functioning of the economy: the ghetto is an exploited subsystem within a larger economy (Fusfeld and Bates 1984; Marable 2015: Marcuse 1996). The ghetto manifests the subordinate social hierarchy of spatially and economically marginalized migrants. This politico-economic approach provides a better understanding of the development and persistence of urban ghettos than the other approaches, notably the assimilationist one. However, it possesses inherent statist and center-oriented viewpoints of migrant enclaves, assuming that a unidirectional influence is exerted from top to bottom and that migrants are trapped in the lowest spatial dimension that the political and economic structure has enforced.

The politico-economic approach influences the advocacy movement to eradicate poverty and social injustice. For instance, in the case of Mae Sot, various NGOs engage in the lives of migrants in their settlements, providing education and healthcare opportunities (Save the Children and World Education 2015). The movement highlights the degradation of migrants, residential segregation, and the social and economic divisions between the minority and the majority. Despite the contribution of the advocacy movement in rectifying social inequality and improving migrants' welfare, it did not adequately recognize that migrants can devise strategies to rebuild their lives, even in precarious conditions. Furthermore, the preoccupation with "segregation" overshadowed the openness of migrant enclaves. Indeed, even ghettos in medieval Europe were not as severed from the outside community as believed (Sennett 1994, cited in Marcuse 1996: 179). It applies to colonial Southeast Asian plural society, as discussed earlier.

Moving away from the obsession with "segregation" and turning attention onto the "openness" of migrant enclaves, the chapter pays attention to the dynamics of migrants carving out their life trajectories and building up social networks in and out of the enclaves. The migrants are indeed segregated, but it is also true that they have connections with the communities outside. Globalization, facilitated by high-tech communication and transport, means migrants' spatial imagination and pursuit of their actual livelihood extend beyond national boundaries. Migrant enclaves are never dead ends; migrants are never spatially incarcerated. Of course, the regulations of their host country can restrict the mobility and connectivity of migrants, particularly those without documents. However, migrants develop coping strategies to continue leading an everyday life and not just stay in state-sanctioned domains: their lives intersect the legal and illegal. The transnational dimension makes migrants' mobility and connectivity more dynamic; migrant enclaves nurture their ability to develop social networks and to imagine and realize their future beyond national boundaries.

The central point of this paper lies in the new spatial configuration of migrant enclaves as "transnational social spaces," on which a significant amount of work has already been undertaken. The interpretation here differs from the conventional one in that the emphasis is on geographical concreteness. The conventional definition is that "transnational social spaces" are "combinations of social and symbolic ties, positions in networks and organizations and networks of organizations that can be found in at least two geographically and internationally distinct places" (Faist 1999: 40). Thus, transnational social spaces are not necessarily associated firsthand with geographical spaces, even though the term "spaces" implies that notion; it is more the case that it is a metaphorical, abstract term referring to ties and networks. In simple terms, transnational social spaces can be constructed without geographical spaces: cyberspaces can be domains for transnational communities and global villages. However, it is an undeniable fact that humans cannot construct their lives without being tied to geographical spaces firsthand. I do not intend to dismiss the metaphorical understanding in current transnational discourses but to call for the importance of geographical concreteness when discussing transnational communities and global villages (Portes 1996a; Levitt 2001). Migrant enclaves can enrich the discussion of transnationalism and "spaces," serving as the embodiment of transnational social spaces; they actualize "globalization from below" (Portes 1996b; Smith and Guarnizo 1998) in a spatial form.

De Genova's (2005) notion of "transnational conjunctural space" provides excellent inspiration for the spatial configuration of migrant enclaves. Mexican migration has been pervasive in Chicago, which leads De Genova to identify the city as *Mexican Chicago*. He sees,

> *Mexican Chicago* as transnational conjunctural space - a Chicago that is practically and materially implicated in Mexico and thus, a Chicago that can be understood to belong meaningfully to Latin American...Not merely "ethnic enclave" or an "immigrant" ghetto, then, Mexican Chicago is a conjuncture of social *relations* and thus comprises innumerable places (2005: 7; italic emphasis original).

Similarly, I regard Mae Sot as *Burmese Mae Sot*; the town strongly associates with Burmese migration and becomes a transnational conjunctural space. By "conjunctural," I mean to demonstrate an interconnected social reality that involves at least two localities. Although physically located in Thailand, *Burmese Mae Sot* belongs meaningfully to Myanmar: it is a conjuncture of the national and the transnational, comprising everyday social interactions and meaningful practices that extend beyond national boundaries. Not merely a migrant ghetto, *Burmese Mae Sot* interlinks the movement of people, money, and ideas across the border.

In this chapter, *Burmese Mae Sot* has two spatial coverages: in the broader sense, it means Mae Sot itself; in a narrower sense, it means migrant settlements in the form of migrant enclaves. Furthermore, transnational conjunctural space applies to both, although the focus will be on the latter.

Transnational conjunctural spaces in Mae Sot are undocumented domains. Thus, the central question is how the settlements can exist at all in the absence of legal approval. Does their presence reveal negligence or weakness on the part of the state? It is certainly not the case. The border is an uncompromising symbol of the state's sovereignty. State's mapping practices centered on the border throughout nation-building, as the seminal work of Thongchai Winichakul (1994) reveals. The state's regulatory authority is in everyday practice in the border towns, and migrants have much to fear as they advance across the border. Scholars, however, have explored how borderlanders navigate the state's regulatory practices (Schoenberger and Turner 2008; Turner 2013; Walker 1999). In line with this approach, the chapter emphasizes the agency of undocumented migrants who constitute their lives in migrant enclaves. This chapter puts forward the argument that the persistence of migrant enclaves as transnational conjunctural spaces, despite the state's interventions, lies in their formation in terms of governance. Migrant enclaves are frequently considered to be devoid of any governance, arising haphazardly as the migrants search for a cheap settlement. They are abandoned ghettos rife with the disorder; governance is unthinkable. However, the findings presented in this chapter suggest that governance—a system in which migrants are regulated under a particular leadership—does exist in migrant enclaves. What makes this governance in these illegal transnational conjunctural spaces possible? It is the migrant schools that run in all the enclaves of Mae Sot. These schools serve administrative units beyond their educational purposes (Ball and Dim 2016; Oh 2016). The schools set up with the cooperation of NGOs, and even Thai locals, in the absence of proper legal status, provide a stable base for an illegal transnational conjunctural space.

Mobility/fluidity is another factor underpinning the persistence of transnational conjunctural spaces, although it is often mistakenly thought to dismantle a social system. However, as Alvarez (1984: 121-122) observes, a border society is based upon people's mobility, which intersects national and transnational boundaries and legal and illegal domains. This fluidity makes migrant enclaves dynamic: as one group of people flows out, another flows in; migrant enclaves are a conjuncture of this ebb and flow.

This conjuncture is not necessarily confined to the movement of migrants between their home and host countries, although this is often a preoccupation in transnational studies. Migrants in Mae Sot certainly do not follow this pattern, their network extending beyond Myanmar and Thailand. Migrant enclaves facilitate this expansion by serving as interconnected nodes across the border and beyond.

By making these three factors (governance, mobility, and connectivity) the focus of this chapter, I redefine migrant enclaves not as segregated areas but as transnational conjunctural spaces.

The Constitution of *Burmese Mae Sot*

Burmese Mae Sot, a transnational conjunctural space practically and materially associated with Myanmar, is not a recent creation. Here let us revisit Mae Sot's geography and its effects. Its geographical location has played a significant role in formulating Mae Sot as a transnational conjunctural space; Mae Sot had "collective destinies" with the neighboring country.

Mae Sot's prominence grew in the latter part of the 1980s when Burmese politics and economy disintegrated, and Burmese people migrated to Mae Sot to seek political sanctuary and economic opportunities. Massive migration from Burma boosted population growth in Mae Sot and changed the economic and social conditions of the town. As of 2016, the total number of Burmese migrants was estimated to be 200,000, among whom registered migrants remained at 64,395 (Gately 2016; IOM 2016: 14). It demonstrates the significance of undocumented migration in Mae Sot.

Massive migration changed the urban landscape: empty spaces across the town transformed into migrant enclaves. Burmese migrants took over the former residences of the local poor. My investigation tells that there were around fifteen migrant enclaves within the town district (Mae Sot municipality) as of 2016. The size of each enclave varied: some contained just a handful of houses; others held more than thirty.

I visited a migrant enclave on the east side of Mae Sot, finding myself baffled with locating it as trees and grass surrounded it, but once through, the most striking feature of the enclave was its formation. About fifteen houses clustered into what resembled a typical Burmese village and a refugee village that I had previously visited; the houses were of a simple style, built mainly from leaves, bamboo, and timber. Most of the residents here came from Thaton in Mon State of Myanmar. Across a small path, a larger enclave accommodated thirty-two households, mainly from Kawkareik in Karen State. This enclave, which also resembled a refugee village, included a migrant school named Hsa Thoo Lei. Its headmaster guided me around the two enclaves and introduced the migrant residents. She acted as a village leader, overseeing community matters such as sanitation and water supply in addition to the education of the migrant; her leadership was evident when she instantly assembled nine people for met to conduct an introductory survey and interviews.

Most households comprised parents and children: the average size of a family was five. Although it was common for grandparents to have remained in Myanmar to tend the agricultural fields and livestock, the family unit, centered on the relationships between parents and children, was maintained. Above all, migrant residents were able to live a village-like lifestyle in the enclaves; some were even equipped with playgrounds where children and youths could play football, volleyball, and sepaktakraw. On my visit to an enclave during *Kathina*,[33] I was fascinated by festival moods where neighbors shared sweets, noodles, rice, and Burmese tea *(Laphet)*. Also, wedding and funeral ceremonies often took place in the enclaves, and residents from neighboring enclaves attended. Such scenes are not in keeping with the commonly held view of migrant ghettos but suggest instead that social ties continue to be nurtured so that migrants continue with their community-centered lives even without legal status.

33 It is a Buddhist festival that comes at the end of the rainy season, usually falling in October.

Not all migrants lived in migrant enclaves, though: most factory workers stayed in dormitories provided by the factory owners; shop employees in shops stayed either in the shops or the shopkeepers' homes; domestic workers also stayed in their employers' homes; and some migrant households were clustered within local Thai residential areas. However, the trend was for suburban residential areas formerly used by Thai people to transform into migrant settlements. For instance, the areas near the United Nations High Commissioner for Refugees (UNHCR) office were inhabited predominantly by local Thais in December 1999. However, in December 2003, I found that migrants had begun to settle there, and by July 2005, the areas primarily became migrant settlements. The establishment of a garment factory drove this transformation. The factory changed a former local Thai residence into a dormitory accommodating Burmese factory workers.

Ethnicity was not a crucial factor in the formation of migrant enclaves: various ethnic groups, including the Burman, the Mon, and the Chin, often lived and associated together. However, the Sgaw Karen, particularly the Christian Sgaw Karen working in Karen organizations such as the Karen Women Organization and the Karen Youth Organization, established their residential settlements, usually in their office complexes. They also have deep relations with refugee camps that host their families and relatives and the Karen organizations mentioned above. In contrast, the Pwo Karen, most of whom are Buddhist, are likely to mingle together with other Burmese in migrant enclaves. Non-ethnic political organizations such as the National League for Democracy also used their offices as living spaces. Of particular note are the Muslim migrants who established their exclusive settlements incorporating their mosques.

It is not that migrants squatted, free of charge, in unclaimed spaces; migrant residents did pay rent to the Thai owners for the use of spaces and buildings. Although the amount of rent varies depending on the types and locations, a single house in migrant enclaves as of 2017 is at least 2,500 baht[34] per month, a substantial increase from 500 - 700 baht in 2005. Since migrants earned the Thai minimum wage of thirty baht per day, which many are not, it was difficult for them to bear the cost. Interestingly, televisions became widespread - there are ways to purloin the electricity - in migrant enclaves, and affluent migrants even purchase a motorcycle, though an old secondhand one.

Migrant enclaves were often subjected to police raids, which presented daily stress; most migrants had been arrested, and some were even forcefully deported to Myawaddy. According to one migrant resident, he bribed the police with 1,000 baht in 2005 to get back a family member under arrest. The expected bribe has now considerably increased to 10,000 baht, which would cause financial devastation for them. When the police raided migrant enclaves, the residents would run away and return later, and this collective escape provided a source of camaraderie among the migrants. They often joked and laughed as they remembered the behaviors of their neighbors when running away.

Although constantly under physical threat from the police and sometimes shattered, these migrant enclaves in non-state-sanctioned spaces survived. Why did they persist? It was because they were not formed haphazardly but based on solid institutions that provided

34 1 USD was equivalent to about 30 baht when the data was collected.

governance to the residents.

Governance in Migrant Enclaves

What makes the case of migrant enclaves in Mae Sot unique—exceptional even compared to other countries—is the presence of migrant schools.[35] Although similar migrant schools exist elsewhere, for instance, the US-Mexico border, European countries, Nigeria, and China (Fong and Murphy 2006; Gobbo 2009; Macias 1996; Umar and Tahir 2009; Van Daele and van Poucke 1984; Weiler 1994), these are mainly government schools, and, in the cases of Nigeria and China, the majority of the migrant students are internal citizens. In contrast, the migrant schools in Mae Sot were established by the migrants in cooperation with NGOs, and the enrolled students are foreign nationals. Moreover, the fact that the schools represent migrant enclaves and act as administrative units is unusual and certainly presents a new understanding of migrants' lives. These schools provide a strong foundation, ensuring stability in migrants' lives, their children's education, and the maintenance of the family unit.

This combination of migrant schools and enclave administration is a recent development dating back to the early 1990s when a handful of hardly noticeable migrant schools were established. However, migrant leaders realized the importance of collaborating among themselves and other partners, eventually forming a representative organization, the Burmese Migrant Workers' Education Committee, in 1999 to promote and advance migrant education. This organization

35 I will comprehensively explore migrant schools in Chapter 5.

played an important role in cooperating with international partners and mobilizing the resources needed to establish migrant schools. Meanwhile, NGOs, which had concentrated on activities inside refugee camps, began to realize that undocumented migrants in the towns also needed humanitarian support and so started to turn their attention to them. As a result of this collaboration, the development of migrant education progressed rapidly, particularly in the mid-2000s.

This growing trend in migrant education is impressive: in the 1990s, migrant schools numbered between two and three, and migrant students around 200. However, this number had significantly increased by 2000 and continued to evolve throughout the 2000s-2010s. A survey done in 2014 (Save the Children and World Education 2015: 16) shows that there were 65 migrant schools and 13,459 students in Mae Sot and its vicinities.[36] As of the early 2020s, the schools run in a similar capacity.[37]

Such growth means that a vital institution has emerged from the migrants' endeavors and collaboration with other partners, despite the absence of proper legal status. Nor are the migrant schools run haphazardly, but they operate in a collective form. They began as unauthorized institutions but developed enough to invite the Thai state to recognize them as "Learning Centers," semi-legal institutions. Democratization in Myanmar (2010-2021) allowed migrant schools in Mae Sot to cooperate with schools inside

---

36 In Thailand, there were 106 schools and 18,312 students in total. The respective number of migrant schools and students in other areas is as follows: 1 and 38 in Bangkok; 3 and 320 in Chiang Mai; 1 and 98 in Chiang Rai; 4 and 780 in Kanchanaburi; 12 and 520 in Phangnga; 1 and 35 in Phetchaburi; 13 and 2,462 in Ranong; and 6 and 600 in Samut Sakorn (Save the Children and World Education 2015: 16).

37 https://www.mecctak2.com/, accessed December 9, 2022.

Myanmar. For instance, I observed in February 2014 that teachers from Myawaddy schools came to Hsa Thoo Lei School to discuss education matters such as curriculum. Hsa Thoo Lei School students went to Myawaddy schools to sit for a matriculation test.

Migrant schools are now profoundly and visibly rooted in almost every migrant enclave. In addition to educational provision, the schools have become socio-cultural bodies where migrants maintain their social ties and engender a sense of belonging, even in the face of precarious conditions. It was a strategic crossroad when migrant leaders reproduced their own culture and acquired external human and financial resources, demonstrating progress in the structure of migrant lives.

Hence, the key issues surrounding migrant schools in Mae Sot do not remain in the educational, such as academic performance, but extend to the governance structure in the residential enclaves. Governance has developed as a result of building institutions: establishing migrant schools marked a turning point in the settlement pattern of migrants in Mae Sot. Migrant enclaves became more institutionalized and secure than in the past when they lacked any firm foundation.

Conventionally, governance is often associated with the state and authorized parties. Governance in the migrant enclaves of Mae Sot, however, is not based on formal or legal structures. Although not conforming to the state's laws and regulations, due to the migrant schools, governance is regularly practiced in the enclaves and embedded within daily life.

As previously stated, governance is a system where the people are administered and regulated under a particular leadership. Leadership is vital in actualizing governance. The headmaster of Hsa Thoo Lei School acted as the village head: she distributed welfare resources provided by international NGOs to residents, coordinated day-care services for children whose parents worked, cared for orphans in the school dormitory, organized sanitary education, and networked with other migrant enclaves, Thai locals, and international partners. The 88 generation[38] of the democratic movement, now middle-aged, also played a leading role in caring for migrants in the enclaves. Just like the headmaster of Hsa Thoo Lei, the 88 generation stayed with the migrants in their enclaves and acted as heads of the village. Many of the migrant schools were under their leadership. Although they had once devoted themselves to purely political issues, they now considered migrant education imperative in promoting community welfare in general.[39]

The migrant schools run a series of joint activities to unite and encourage cooperation among the migrants, which has helped to establish the schools as "official" institutions. If this were not the case, each school would run separate, individual learning programs, and migrant education would not be the collective institution it is today. Inter-school cooperation includes school health meetings where the leaders draw up plans for health and sanitary education;

---

38 It refers to the groups of people, usually students, who participated in the democratic movements of 1988 in Myanmar.

39 Inside Myanmar, in particular border areas, ethnic political organizations such as the Karen National Union run their schools to promote ethnic identity. Christian missionaries and Buddhist monks in Myanmar also run religious schools. However, migrant schools in Mae Sot do not intend to promote specific ethnic identity or religious beliefs but to emphasize Burmese national identity and adaptation to Thai society. Indeed, the combination of various ethnic groups in the schools promotes specific ethnic or religious identities impossible. Even migrant schools such as Hsa Thoo Lei that ethnic Karen leaders run do not/cannot promote Karen identity due to ethnic combination within the schools.

monthly training sessions where NGO trainers instruct migrant teachers on how to teach; seminars and conferences on children's rights and the development of children's leadership; and sports activities and cultural performances. For instance, I observed many inter-school activities during the Christmas season: the children enjoyed playing matches, such as volleyball and football, against other schools; supporters from each school exhilaratingly cheered for their teams; award ceremonies took place at the end of the competition. Whenever these joint events happened, migrant enclaves were filled with clapping, laughing, and cheering from students, teachers, parents, and NGO workers; and Burmese and even Thai vendors were selling ice cream, snacks, tea, and betel.

Such instances indeed challenge the belief that anything meaningful hardly takes place in migrant enclaves, given their vulnerability and desperate situation to survive. On the contrary, these joint activities demonstrate how the enclaves are regulated and linked under a central leadership, providing education and complete governance. By taking advantage of such governance, migrants can build their lives inside and outside the enclaves. Without governance based on migrant education, migrant enclaves would have been fragile, and solidarity would have been weak. With this governance, migrants' lives are sustained even without proper legal status.

Mobility, Connectivity, and Multifocal Transnational Trajectories

Transnationalism is deeply embedded in migrants' lives. They were mobile even before settling in Mae Sot, which they would not have reached without courage and strong determination. Mobility is never accidental but is developed and calculated as a product of a person's life course. Mobility becomes seminal when people cross the border. A new reality opens up; they now have to live as undocumented migrants, facing day-to-day threats from the authorities in their host country. Migrant enclaves provide them with sanctuary, but they are not dead ends. The enclaves nurture and develop migrants' mobility and connectivity so that they can see the possibilities of beginning a new life. Migrant enclaves serve as nodes connecting the different journeys in a migrant's life trajectory.

I met Poe Poe[40] in February 2005 when she was staying with her husband and three-year-old son in a migrant enclave near the UNHCR office. She came to Mae Sot in 1997 and met her husband in 1999. Originally, Poe Poe was born in Bathein in 1959 in Myanmar. After completing her high school education, she went to Yangon, where she took a correspondent degree course in physics and obtained a bachelor's degree in 1985. She then worked as an accountant at a university for nine years until she lost her job after participating in the 1988 democratic uprising. Desperate to leave Myanmar, Poe Poe managed to get a passport with help from a sailor friend of her future husband. At first, she intended to go to the USA to attend a conference and continue to stay there, but the meeting was canceled, and so was her plan to leave her home country.

Nevertheless, she kept looking for opportunities abroad and decided on Bangkok. From there, she continued her journey, migrating to Singapore on a student visa in 1991. Poe Poe worked

40 The names in the book are pseudonyms unless they are officially known.

first in a stationery factory, then in a Sony factory producing cassette players, and finally in a computer chip factory in Jurong while staying in Toa Payoh. While working in Singapore, her wages increased from a few hundred Singapore dollars in her first job to 1,500 at the computer chip factory. However, as she had already renewed her student visa once and was unable to do so again, Poe Poe had no option but to return to Myanmar in 1996. On arrival, her passport was confiscated, and she could not obtain another. However, she continued to search for a way to journey overseas once more, and advised by her aunt living in Mae Sot, Poe Poe eventually crossed the border by boat and arrived there in 1997. She was trained and made a living as a hairdresser but could not earn enough money to meet living expenses and hence had to rely on her aunt. However, when her aunt left for the USA, her situation worsened: the cost of a haircut was only twenty baht per person, and although working at home, she only had three or four customers per week. Consequently, Poe Poe attempted to contact the UNHCR and nearby refugee camps to be registered as a refugee. When I met her in 2005, she had not yet been registered as a refugee, but on my return to Mae Sot in 2009, Poe Poe and her family had already left Mae Sot and resettled in the USA.

This story illustrates the transnational life trajectory of a migrant, beginning in Myanmar to Bangkok, to Singapore, back to Myanmar, to Mae Sot, and to the USA. Before migrating to Mae Sot, Poe Poe had already had overseas experiences as political and economic hardship in her home country prompted her to seek opportunities abroad. Then, again struggling to survive in Mae Sot, she found another opportunity to go abroad. For Poe Poe, Mae Sot was a conjuncture of Myanmar, Thailand, and the USA. The main emphasis of transnational studies often lies in the bifocality of migrants, namely that migrants' ties are constructed and maintained only between their home country and host country (Aguilar 2012). However, Poe Poe's story shows that Burmese migrants in Mae Sot are not necessarily tied into this circuit pattern; their journeys can take other directions. They have multifocality in imaging, scaling, and actualizing their transnational trajectory.

This multifocality does not just incorporate foreign countries; Bangkok also has an important position. Migrants travel to Bangkok relatively easily due to social networks and brokerage with Thai police. While socializing in the tea shops of migrant enclaves in Mae Sot, Burmese migrants share and circulate job opportunities in Bangkok and news about their friends already working there. Migrants in Mae Sot take Bangkok as an extended living space in their minds. Their mobility, which has developed throughout their life course, spurs them to embark on the journey to Bangkok. Indeed, throughout my stay, the phenomenon of migrants leaving for Bangkok has been prominent.

On the one hand, it negatively affects local Thai employers. Padadon, a farm owner, lamented on June 27, 2005, that "Mae Sot is like a kindergarten for the Burmese where they learn how to adapt to Thai society. It is here where they learn Thailand's basic language and culture before leaving for big places like Bangkok." It is rare for migrants to bring their children to Bangkok; instead, they put them into dormitories like those at Hsa Thoo Lei or send them to their grandparents in Myanmar. The multifocal lives of the migrants do bring difficulties: their children are neglected; some are deceived by brokers and end up in different locations, such as Pattani in southern Thailand. The case occurred to Poe Poe's husband, who was forced to work in a fishery with monthly wages confiscated by brokers.

Nevertheless, the Bangkok dream is irresistible. In migrant enclaves, tales of *Burmese Bangkok*—a Bangkok deeply rooted in the lives of migrants there—are told and retold, imagined and reimagined: some parts based on reality, other parts distorted. Bangkok is practically and imaginatively placed in migrants' everyday lives. Migrants' lives intersect the migrant enclaves and Bangkok, rescaling them as places on a single continuum, which extends even further to other countries as their transnational trajectories advance. Migrant enclaves act as nodes, constantly exposed to the ebb and flow of people but never dismantled by it. Instead, the continual changes turn the enclaves into dynamic, transnational conjunctural spaces where migrants' multifocal life trajectories develop, cross, and take new shapes.

Conclusion

This chapter has challenged the pathological viewpoint of migrant enclaves, whereby they have been equated to ghettos, a term that carries dark connotations of poverty, crime, and deviation. Above all, migrant enclaves have been regarded as "segregated" places where interaction with the outside world is not supposed to, and indeed cannot, take place. In contrast to this conventional thinking, this chapter has focused on migrants as agents and migrant enclaves as transnational social spaces in an attempt to identify enclaves more specifically with the notion of transnational conjunctural spaces that De Genova (2005) puts forward. The migrant enclaves are the conjunctures of Myanmar and Thailand. Mae Sot has consistently been implicated in Myanmar. *Burmese Mae Sot* belongs not just to Thailand but also to Myanmar. Thus, the two countries intersect in the migrant enclaves.

I have explored the making of transnational conjunctural spaces throughout history. Geographical conditions have been a significant factor in shaping the history of Mae Sot, ensuring that it has had a collective destiny with Myanmar. It was in the late 1980s that a sudden and massive cross-border migration from Myanmar to Mae Sot took place, one peculiar result of which was the widespread formation of migrant enclaves, changing the town's landscape. Migrant enclaves are illegal domains exposed to physical threats from the state authorities. However, they continue to exist and provide sanctuary for Burmese migrants. Such persistence can be explained by governance, whereby migrants are administered and regulated under a particular leadership.

When investigating the cornerstone of this governance, I have highlighted migrant schools. They came into existence in the early 1990s and continued to develop through the collective effort of migrants and cooperation with international partners. This collaboration carried and strengthened migrant education in the face of the state's regulatory activities. These migrant schools in the enclaves act as not only educational institutions but also administrative units; school leaders, who also act as heads of the enclaves, implement governance and promote the welfare of migrants. This governance provides migrants with a solid foundation to build their lives and pursue further opportunities elsewhere.

Mobility and connectivity are catalysts in forming migrant enclaves as transnational conjunctural spaces. Migrants were already mobile before arriving in Mae Sot, as evident in the case of Poe Poe. In the migrants' constant pursuit of better lives, migrant enclaves facilitate their passage from Myanmar through Mae Sot to Bangkok and other countries. Transcending bifocal attentions between their home and adopted countries predominating in conventional transnational studies, these migrants imagine, practice, and actualize a multifocal dimension in their transnational lives. Within the migrant enclaves, Bangkok and other countries come as places on a single continuum; they are the conjunctures of Myanmar, Bangkok, and other countries. Thus, the enclaves are never segregated ghettos, but the places where intersections of time (the past, present, and future) and place (Myanmar, Thailand, and other countries) occur. It is the enclaves that turn migrants' dreams and imagination into reality and that rescale migrants' transnational life trajectories.

Chapter 4

Behind the Scenes: Smuggling in the Borderland

Introduction

Somsak, a local Thai trader, informed me one day that the Bank of Thailand (BOT) would give a presentation on border trade at the Mae Sot Hill Hotel, the most luxurious hotel in town. I rode my motorbike to the hotel the following day to attend the event.[41] Professionally dressed officials of the BOT were delivering a presentation on the border trade, using colorful slides full of figures and statistics. Somsak, sitting next to me, whispered, "It is very superficial. They just show numbers and can't go into the complexity of border trade. Local researchers, or even I myself, could do better research on that with the money the BOT has spent." During the break, Ekamon, another local businessman engaged in border trade since the early 1970s, said to me openly, "They are wasting money on useless things. People from the outside do not know about the border trade here. They can't see the border trade behind the scenes."

The criticism that both Somsak and Ekamon expressed prompts us to examine the local practices of the border trade, the behind-the-scenes trade, which cannot be captured in numbers. For the local traders, behind-the-scenes activity is legitimate, though invisible and at times illegal in the eyes of the state. Statist approaches that differentiate between the official and the unofficial, the legal and the illegal, dismissing the latter as marginal and often pathological, fail to appreciate the normalcy of the border trade that intersects the two areas. Overcoming the formal-informal dichotomy, I show how this nexus of the two sides is played out, how the localized, situated normalcy has its social dynamics and rationalities, its pragmatism

41 This took place on March 31, 2005.

and regulatory apparatus, and how it often defies state-centered notions of legality and/or illegality.

This chapter first builds upon scholars' work in the Southeast Asian borderlands. Conventionally, the primary concern of border studies is to investigate a state's mapping practices and their impact on local societies, including ethnic groups, throughout nation-building (Leach 1964 [1954]; Keyes 1979; Thongchai 1994; Wijeyewardene 1990). Recently, scholars have emphasized the local practices and agencies that produce and use the border (Baird 2010; Dudley 2011; Horstmann and Wadley 2006; Ishikawa 2010; Lamb 2014). The scholarship on border trade epitomizes this approach, highlighting local traders' various strategies for navigating the state's regulatory practices across the border (Endres 2014; Schoenberger and Turner 2008; Tagliacozzo 2005; Turner 2010; 2013; Walker 1999). This chapter, with the case of the Thailand-Myanmar border, is in line with this approach. However, it attempts to shed more light on how local networks and practices, including those built upon ethnic networks, have shaped notions of informality or smuggling so that they are a part of everyday life. In particular, this chapter attempts to demonstrate the intertwined threads of intimacy, commodity, and ethnicity that constitute border trade in the local context, moving across the formal-informal nexus.

Smuggling in the Thailand-Myanmar borderland must also be understood as a part of regional integration processes that have transformed border towns into economic hubs and gateways under the Greater Mekong Subregion (GMS) (ADB 2001; 2004; 2012a).[42] One of the policy-makers' priorities concerns facilitating

42 The East-West Economic Corridor connects between Da Nang in Vietnam and

cross-border trade as regulated by the states (ADB 2012b: 4-5). Meanwhile, scholars critically review these border development projects' impact on border societies, including migrant laborers and local governments (Arnold and Hewison 2005; Lin and Grundy-Warr 2012; Maneepong 2010; Swe and Chambers 2011). Although revealing the local dimensions of state-driven projects, such scholars have been limited in accounting for why informal ways of life have persisted against the state's aspirations and how they perceive the dynamics of the nexus of the formal and informal actions and behaviors in these border societies.

Understanding the persistence of the unauthorized movement of goods and people requires a consideration of the geographical, historical, and cultural conditions of the border town. Mae Sot, located between the ocean and the inland area, has long served as a hub for trade. It has enjoyed an autonomy fostered by a power vacuum in the premodern period. Although the modern nation-state has attempted to regulate cross-border trade, smuggling as a cultural practice has remained deeply ingrained. Interfaces between the different scales and intents of state and local traders have turned smuggling into a contested and dynamic form throughout the years. How can we account for this dynamic?

My theoretical position primarily develops from the integrative study on the informal economy (Castells and Portes 1989; Portes and Haller 2005; Van Schendel and Abraham 2005). I identify three approaches that have emerged since the 1970s within the study of the informal economy: social marginality, state regulation, and small

---

Mawlamyine in Myanmar via Mae Sot and Mukdahan in Thailand and Savannakhet in Laos.

firms approaches (Cheng and Gereffi 1994). The social marginality approach—namely, the ILO or structural approach—emphasizes that a shortage of employment opportunities/surplus of labor supply in modern urban sectors triggers various informal survival strategies not integrated into the formal economy (ILO 2013). In contrast, the state regulation approach stresses the avoidance of burdensome state regulations and integration or deep linkages with the formal economy (Castells and Portes 1989). The small firms approach emphasizes the agency and social embeddedness of informal economic activities. It is concerned with "how people mobilize resources and overcome barriers through reciprocal ties (e.g., ethnic networks) not only to survive but also to grow and prosper" (Cheng and Gereffi 1994: 194-219). I build upon both the state regulation and small firms approach because, unlike in the social marginality approach, people in the informal sector, in this case, are not marginalized, whereas smuggling while avoiding state regulation is well integrated into the formal economy; and above all, people effectively employ their local knowledge, mobility, and ethnic networks.

I downplay sectoral divisions between the formal and informal in line with the state regulation approach. The two parts cannot operate separately in a real sense because ontologically, "order creates disorder," and "the formal economy creates its own informality," as Lomniz (1988: 54) mentions. Indeed the notion of formality and informality is a product of the state's regulatory practices. Portes and Haller (2005: 409) point out the paradox of state control, stating that "official efforts to obliterate unregulated activities through the proliferation of rules and controls often expand the very conditions that give rise to these activities." Focusing on the formal only is problematic because the category is fluid and situational across time and space. What is formal/legal in one country may be informal/illegal in another; likewise, what is informal/illegal at one time may be formal/legal in another (Tannenbaum and Durrengerger 1990). Transnational movements of goods are often subject to this fluidity and arbitrariness, given that neighboring states apply different legal standards to the same goods.

This situation calls for an alternative distinction that allows for social acceptance beyond state-centric categorization. In this respect, my thought is aligned with an idea from Abraham and van Schendel (2005: 4), which discerns between the "licit"—that is to say, what is socially acceptable and legitimate—and the "illicit"—that is, what is otherwise.[43] The licit is deeply associated with the customs and culture of a locality. It constitutes "normalcy," although it may at times be illegal in state law. Smuggling is an example of illegal but licit.[44] It represents a way of life in border societies, which was present long before the advent of the state into the borderlands. As Baud and van Schendel (1997) observe, local state agencies are often part of this practice.

Although Abraham and van Schendel and others suggest the helpful concept of licitness to overcome state-centric categorization, they do not much note convergences in the "small firms" or "local networks" approach in their discussion of informality. I aim to fill this gap by emphasizing how people mobilize their geographical and cultural resources and overcome barriers through local networks

43 Van Schendel stands on his earlier scholarship on smuggling on the Ganges. See Willem van Schendel (1993).

44 In contrast, human trafficking and smuggling of human organs are illegal and illicit since they violate state law and are socially unacceptable.

so that their unauthorized cross-border trade can become licit and legitimate in their everyday lives. Here, I point out intimacy, commodity, and ethnicity as crucial factors that enable people to navigate the formal-informal nexus. They avoid state regulatory practices by employing deep-rooted geographical and cultural knowledge of the borderland. At the same time, the exchange of commodities, driven by the principle of comparative advantage across the border, validates the presence of local mediators, even though unauthorized. In particular, ethnic networks have a long history as players in the pivotal role of moving goods across the border in cooperation with local traders and even state agencies.

My study demonstrates the social dynamics of the cross-border movements that involve different social groups, such as neighboring states, individual traders, and ethnic groups. It reveals the power geometry between social groups concerning flows and movements, as Massey (1991) notes. Borders are constructed, demarcated, and crossed in everyday contingent encounters, wherein players try to claim and negotiate their "entitlement" and exercise their situated agencies. Local worlds undergo transformation processes under the influence of state regimes, ethnic politics, commodity flows, and local power dynamics. During these processes, a new ordering of the borders emerges. The state and other social groups—such as smugglers and ethnic political groups—participate, contest, and negotiate. This interaction forms a new order with its regulatory practices that make border trade possible with a combination of the formal and the informal (Chang 2004; 2009; Toyota 2003; Walker 1999).

Building upon this perspective, the chapter first provides a historical background showing that black markets have long been rampant along the border. It then demonstrates how smuggling is a way of life deeply rooted in the particular locality. Next is a discussion of the cross-border movement of goods as part of the formal-informal mix. Finally, I will show how the ordering of the borderland has taken shape in the participation of ethnic political groups.

Historical Development of Informal Border Trade

I briefly revisit the historical background to understand the current practice of informal border trade. As mentioned in Chapter 2, smuggling at present is a direct legacy of the massive black markets in the Thailand-Myanmar borderland that operated from the early 1960s to the late 1980s. When the Burmese military seized power in 1962, they projected "the Burmese Way to Socialism," which drove Myanmar to self-isolation. All private-sector organizations and property were nationalized and confiscated. The closed-door policy of the military regime caused a scarcity of consumer goods in the country, leading to the establishment of black markets in the borderland, particularly in the areas near Mae Sot, under the guidance of the KNU.

The black markets' impact on Myanmar's national economy during those days was enormous. Although the exact figures are not available, estimates of the illegal trade vary between 50 and 85 percent of the total official trade in the mid-1980s. According to Khin Maung Nyunt, nearly two-thirds of the goods sold on the black market of Myanmar were smuggled in from Thailand, and the total illegal trade was thought to have a turnover of up to 50 percent of the official trading (Khin Maung Nyunt 1988: 94).

The effects of the black markets on the previously sleepy outpost of Mae Sot were dramatic. The town was rapidly transformed into a bustling new market town, primarily because it was the center for much of this new trade. This change triggered domestic migration, mainly by business people from Bangkok, who were primarily Chinese (Anurak 1998: 17). The black market also involved massive participation by the Burmese in transporting goods to the inner parts of Burma. KNU soldiers protected their journey. By engaging in border trade, people across the border developed a strong sense of collective identity, regardless of nationality. As the two neighboring states were limited in controlling the space, they enjoyed relative autonomy under the auspices of the para-state organization, the KNU. The borderland remained a non-state space in which unofficial movements of people and goods prevailed and where the division of nationalities became irrelevant.

The Thailand-Myanmar borderland witnessed significant geopolitical and geoeconomic changes in the late 1980s, when the military regime drove the economy of Myanmar into an abysmal situation (Smith 1999a: 24). Anti-government demonstrations, beginning in March 1988, were soon rampant throughout the country. The political crisis finally led to the introduction of a refashioned military regime through a coup in September 1988. The new military regime attempted to restore the country to a normal state by suppressing democratic uprisings.

Meanwhile, the new junta officially discarded the defunct closed-door economic policy and began promoting an open-door policy, particularly with neighboring countries. It attempted to formalize trade and political relations with these countries by nullifying the operations of the black markets. As Myanmar and Thailand began to formalize their political and economic relations, and Burmese troops increasingly encroached upon the borderland, the previously thriving black markets near Mae Sot unavoidably suffered a steep decline, as was evident by the late 1980s. Because the Burmese government developed Myawaddy as its official trading outpost in the late 1980s, Thai business people began to send their export goods through Myawaddy posts rather than through the black markets. By 1992, the last black markets overseen by the KNU in Wangkha and Phalu had become obsolete. However, the closure of the black markets motivated former black-market merchants to operate in Mae Sot. The town became a central marketplace rather than an outpost for the black markets, inheriting the legacy of these markets.

The two states attempted to make border trade official and, as part of the attempts, completed the Thai-Myanmar Friendship Bridge connecting Myawaddy and Mae Sot in 1997. However, the bridge has remained symbolic. In practice, regulation of the border trade between the two states has not been fully achieved. The capacity of the states is limited in controlling the porous border. For the Myanmar side, not the state agency but an ethnic group, the Democratic Karen Buddhist Army (DKBA), which split from the KNU in 1994 and which has been collaborating with the Myanmar government since then, has been in charge of border trade (Lintner 1999: 413-414). Order along the border is not dominated by the states but managed by other players, including unauthorized merchants and the DKBA. Smuggling lies in the dynamics of the creation of a contested and collective order. Partly accepted and partly rejected, it makes the transaction and transition of goods across the border possible. It is not necessarily clandestine, nor does its illegality necessarily preclude its contribution to the operation of border trade.

Smuggling as *Withi Chiwit*

"*Phi, buri ao mai?*" (Brother, do you want tobacco?) "*Whiskey ao mai?*" (Do you want whiskey?) Whenever I rode to the bank of the Moei River, which flows along the border, a band of Burmese vendors speaking fluent Thai would approach and surround my motorbike, enticing me to buy contraband items, especially cigarettes and liquor. They are routinely stationed under the Thai-Myanmar Friendship Bridge to wait for passersby. Traveling farther along the riverbank to the north, one is overwhelmed at the sight of some one hundred unauthorized merchants selling garlic, chili, onion, crab, shrimp, dried fish, sunglasses, souvenir items, and other goods to domestic and foreign tourists, as well as to local Thai customers and retailers from downtown Mae Sot.

Interestingly enough—and paradoxically—border patrol soldiers are usually stationed among them, and customs officials may at times be spotted strolling through these markets. Next to the traders is a roofed official border market, Talat Rim Moei (Moei Market), which carries electronic goods, confectionaries, wooden souvenirs, guitars, gems, and clothes. The landscape of the river bank thus shows the ironic but stable coexistence of the smugglers, the soldiers, and the official market.

<Photo 1> **Burmese Vendors along the Riverbank**

Source: Author

I felt compelled to discover what the customs office thinks of these unauthorized merchants. To this end, I visited the office and asked the chief officer whether he charged them taxes and why he did not expel them. He replied, "They do not pay any tax to us. If we take action against them, they just run away. Once we leave, they come back. We cannot capture them. They are what is known as free traders."[45] Later, I went to the customs office again and talked to the vice chief officer, to whom I posed a similar question. He replied, "It is *withi chiwit* (a "way of life" in Thai). It is like a traditional thing. We just allow them to do that because this is minimal but crucial for their lives. At present, we try to keep the number of merchants from growing."[46] Much later, when revisiting the office and chatting

45 Chief Officer of the Mae Sot customs office, interview, Mae Sot, June 28, 2005.

46 Vice Chief Officer of the Mae Sot customs office, interview, Mae Sot, December 6,

with a lower-level official, I received a similar answer from him.[47] Regardless of the ranking of the official or the time of day, this attitude did not waver. It demonstrates that smuggling is tenacious and associated with the tradition of the border locality such that it is accepted as *withi chiwit* even by state agencies in general.

Indeed, smuggling is *withi chiwit* for the Burmese merchants. Ali, a vendor selling sunglasses, rings, and souvenirs, told me, "I do business here to support my wife and three children. I have been here for seven years. I could go to Malaysia, where I worked before I got married. But I want to live with my family in Myawaddy." For him, smuggling is a deliberate way to live and lets him support his family. Another vendor selling souvenirs, Hlaing Zaw said, "I worked in a factory in Nakhonsawan for four years before I started this job. I also lived for some time in a refugee camp with my mother. But I didn't like living under those restricted conditions and started doing this because I wanted freedom." Like Ali and Hlaing Zaw, many Burmese merchants take up smuggling as a rational choice for their life trajectories. The Thai side of the border has become the field in which they pursue their livelihoods.

They do not haphazardly situate themselves on the border; instead, a community has been formed among them. The riverbank is for conducting business, but a resting place is behind it. There they play cards, drink tea and coffee, and take care of the children whose parents are by the riverbank or have gone to Bangkok to work. They have a regular life cycle, which typically begins with their arrival on the Thai side as early as 6:00 a.m. and ends with

2005

47 An official of the Mae Sot customs office, interview, Mae Sot, February 21, 2011.

their return to Myawaddy at around 6:00 p.m. However, border-crossing patterns are not standardized: some people cross the bridge, passing through the immigration checkpoints of the two countries on a one-day border pass, whereas others cross by boat. Although they do not pay taxes to the Thai authorities, they pay taxes on the Burmese side to the DKBA, which is in charge of border-crossing points.[48] They usually pay 100 kyat per person and approximately 150 to 200 additional kyat for goods, depending on the size of their merchandise shipment. On the Thai side, they pay twenty baht to rent a sizeable sun-blocking parasol from local Thai individuals.

Their goods come from various areas of Myanmar: fresh and dried fish are from Mawlamyine; dried chilies, tobacco, and alcohol from Yangon; fresh vegetables from Myawaddy; and manufactured goods, such as sunglasses and rings, are made in China but transported from Yangon. Some merchants even carry Russian Viagra and Japanese sex DVDs. The amount of daily revenue made from these goods ranges from 300 to 500 baht.

Smuggled goods are well integrated into the economic system of Mae Sot. In particular, such goods as dried chilies, onions, and dried fish are mainly supplied to the town by riverbank merchants. Local Thai retailers regularly come to the border to buy goods sold at higher prices in the markets in town. For example, in the mid-2000s, the price of onions per kilogram at the riverbank was around ten baht, whereas it was higher by two to five baht in town. Individual Thais come to the riverbank as regular customers to buy these goods from the smugglers. Thus, this practice is part of the everyday lives

48 The DKBA's involvement in border trade will be explained in detail later in the section "The Ordering of the Border."

of the local Thai population.

On the one hand, the smugglers use their mobility to avoid regulatory actions from the state, but on the other hand, they also position themselves deep within the border landscape. My observations during the erection of a wall attest to the symbiotic relationship between the smugglers and the border. Initially, the merchants were located on an islet in the Moei River.[49] In early April 2005, state authorities began constructing a wall along the Thai side of the riverbank in order to prevent floods. However, it was apparent that it was also intended to prevent Burmese vendors from advancing into the inner areas. During its construction, I noticed that the ferroconcrete wall, which stretched along the riverbank, was a complete mismatch with the natural landscape of the border, an indication of abuse by the state. As the wall continued to rise, I went to the riverbank as often as possible to observe how the vendors would survive, given this blocking wall. It was striking that they persistently crossed over the wall at every stage of the construction.

When the wall was finished months later, it was not as ugly as it had been during its construction. People stroll along the path beside the wall equipped with benches and lamps. The vendors have positioned themselves along the wall, building their new stalls out of wood to match the height of the wall. Some have even set up shop inside the path, resiliently appropriating the new edifice. The border is packed with many people, and the Burmese vendors enjoy even more tourists

49 Initially, the islet was in the middle of the river without any land connection to either side of the riverbank. However, during the process of building the Friendship Bridge, the islet became contiguous with the Thai side of the riverbank. Subsequently, the Burmese people exploited the land for cultivating crops and setting up vending stalls. Some Burmese also built makeshift houses. For details, see Maung Aung Myoe (2002: 113) and Bangkok Post (2005b).

and customers than in the past. Throughout the construction of the wall, the vendors have kept themselves tied to the border, regardless of how the state attempted to change its landscape. Flynn (1997) has noted that the Shabe border residents of West Africa claim, "We are the border!" to maintain their freedom of movement and economic opportunities in the face of the controlling practices of the state. Similarly, the Burmese vendors have come to embody the border and to appropriate the state's involvement to their advantage. Their deep connection and intimacy with the border over time have enabled them to transcend the wall, which attempted to block them from it. As van Schendel (2005a: 61) notes, "Their power is based on a detailed knowledge of topography, social fields, and overlapping scales that allows objects and persons to navigate the border safely."

The *withi chiwit* of the smugglers has been carved out by these encounters with the state and their constant adaptation to changing conditions. During this process, the vendors have rescaled their imaginary and practical boundaries and have redesigned their daily lives in symbiosis with the border landscape.

Bridge and Boat

As mentioned earlier, the Thai-Myanmar Friendship Bridge was completed in 1997 as an attempt by the two states to make the border trade official. The bridge was therefore expected to become the main channel for the cross-border passage of goods. In addition, the movement of goods by boat was expected to cease at the crossing points along the river. However, contrary to expectations, I observed that sizable portions of goods continued to arrive at river piers by boat. Why has this state of affairs persisted? Aside from a cultural understanding that this long-existing practice has been accepted as "licit" in its context, we need to explore the answer further by looking at Myanmar's political economy.

As mentioned above, the Myanmar government initiated an open-door policy in the late 1980s. It subsequently developed Myawaddy as a point for bilateral trade with Thailand to make trading patterns official by replacing the black markets along the border. The construction of the Thai-Myanmar Friendship Bridge was a product of these endeavors. Indeed, the bridge symbolically marked a turning point in the history of the border.

However, the government's policy was not a full-scale open-door policy. As an underdeveloped country, Myanmar needed to protect and nurture some of its industrial sectors until it could develop them to a certain standard. Thus, the country adopted a policy restricting the import of certain items. At the same time, Myanmar was sanctioned by other countries, notably the US and European countries, because of human rights violations relative to democratic movements. Hence, the export of goods from these countries to Myanmar was banned, a move that dwarfed the initial hope for open and official trade and led to the scarcity of some goods that were essential to the daily lives of ordinary Burmese people.

Notable restricted items included seasoning powder (*ajinomoto*, MSG), beverages (particularly Coca-Cola), biscuits, chewing gum, cakes, wafers, chocolates, canned food, rice noodles, liquor, beer, tobacco, fresh fruits, and plastic products.[50] Consequently, these

50 The list of items was acquired from the Tak Chamber of Commerce and the Mae Sot Customs Office.

goods had to enter Myanmar not via the bridge but through the boat piers. An interesting fact is that the export of these items from the Thai side was well recorded and legalized by the Mae Sot customs office; however, importing these items was unofficial and not legalized by Burmese customs authorities. Here, we see the ironic integration of the legal/official on the Thai side with the illegal/unofficial on the Burmese side, as legal standards apply differently to the same goods.

In a typical daily scene, boats busily carry cargo across the river, and Burmese porters load and unload them at river piers. Local traders and customs officials estimate that more than sixty percent of the export volume goes to the Burmese side by boat and that around fifty percent of the import volume arrives at the Thai side by boat.

<Photo 2> Border Trade by Boat

Source: Author

This practice is evidence of the incapacity of the customs offices in the two countries to regulate the movement of goods across the porous border. A customs official in Mae Sot explained that the office had to cover three provinces—Tak, Kamphengphet, and Sukhothai—so it could not have close control over the movement of all goods across the border. However, the export volume from Thailand to Myanmar has been relatively well recorded, as exported items have not been taxed to promote exports. Thai exporters, in general, tend to conform to the regulations set by the customs office. However, because the customs office imposes taxes on imported items—a 30 percent customs tax and a 7 percent VAT in the mid-2000s, depending on the type of product—Thai importers have been reluctant to report import transactions to the office.

Moreover, the actions of the customs office are not always consistent, as illustrated by the following incident. According to one report (Irrawaddy 2004), officials from the Mae Sot customs office seized 309 sacks of Burmese rice smuggled to the Thai side. Sometimes, Burmese rice traders on the border pay off Thai officials so that they will allow contraband rice to enter the country. Thai traders then carry the contraband grain into the interior provinces. The report includes a statement from a Burmese trader: "But sometimes they [customs officials] don't take our money and seize our rice instead." The trader went on to complain that Thai authorities often seize Burmese rice at the river as it enters the country, but then they allow Thai traders to transport the rice to the inner parts of the country without conflict. He says, "It is just to show that customs is preventing the smuggling of Burmese rice into Thailand." This incident demonstrates the inconsistency of the customs office. While customs officials acknowledge smuggling as a cultural practice, they at times engage in dealings under the table, taking "tea money" from the traders. This incident also shows that the categorization of "smuggled items" is negotiable and that, through such negotiation, smuggled items can be integrated into the entire circulation system.

The customs office has often played a role in facilitating border trade. The head of the customs office boasted that one of his main accomplishments was the establishment of warehouses along the border to cater to traders' logistics needs. However, by building these warehouses, the office also intended to track and control the movement of items, which local traders consider a disturbance. Ekamon stated, "What they need to do is just to let local people trade in their own ways. When we need help, then they can assist us. But now they try to control us. It only disturbs us."

The following table on the trade volume presents a general picture of border trade.

<Table 1> Volume of Exports and Imports Recorded at the Mae Sot Customs Office (2008-2012) (Unit: 1 million baht)

Year	Exports	Imports
2008	17,513	1,236
2009	22,175	1,714
2010	28,673	1,110
2011	17,492	855
2012	33,969	1,163

* Thai fiscal year begins on October 1 and ends on September 30.
Source: Mae Sot Customs Office

As listed in Table 1, export volumes are much higher than import volumes. This difference, I suggest, elicits two points, one explicit and the other implicit. The explicit point, which can be plainly observed, is that Thailand dominates by far in border trade. The implicit point is that exported goods are generally well-recorded, whereas imported goods are not well-checked. As mentioned earlier, Thai customs authorities do not tax exported goods to boost exports. Hence, Thai exporters do not necessarily attempt to bypass the customs office. However, because imported goods are taxed, traders attempt to evade the customs office with their imports.

<Table 2> Major Export and Import Items through the Mae Sot Customs Office in 2012

(Unit: 1 million baht)

Exports		Imports	
Item	Amount	Item	Amount
Gasoline	2,806	Buffalo alive	305
Beer	2,198	Wood furniture	300
Cloth	1,344	Antimony mineral	110
Cooking oil	1,254	Dried fish maw	33
TV	1,125	Sesame	31
Seasoning powder (MSG)	905	Fish	30
Diesel oil	883	Charcoal	18
Instant coffee	756	Used bicycle	17
Motorbike	668	Broken-milled rice	16
Biscuit	601	Cashew Nut	15

Source: Mae Sot Customs Office Website

Table 2 presents some contrasts between export and import items. The exported items primarily include consumer goods (beer, cloth, MSG). In contrast, livestock, fish, and agricultural products are the main imported items. These differences demonstrate that comparative advantage governs border trade, wherein the Thai side is more competitive in consumer and manufactured items and the Myanmar side in agricultural products. Interestingly, although such items as beer, seasoning powder, and biscuits are not allowed into Myanmar by the Myanmar government, they are significant items entering Myanmar. These items are legally recorded on the Thai side but are illegal and thus smuggled on the Myanmar side. Thus, it illustrates how the illegal and the legal intersect in the cross-border movement of goods as the two states apply different legal standards to the same goods.

In Table 1, one may wonder why both export and import volumes suddenly plummeted in 2011. This change is related to political conditions in Myanmar. Myanmar closed the official border-crossing points between Mae Sot and Myawaddy from July 18, 2010 to December 4, 2011, in protest against a river embankment construction project and in preparation for a general election on November 7, 2010, and the ensuing political restructuring (Bangkok Post 2011). During this period, virtually all exported and imported goods were smuggled on the Myanmar side. However, on the Thai side, these goods were traded officially and thus recorded by the customs office. It shows that even if Myanmar closes its doors, goods will move through unofficial points on the Myanmar side.

The impact of political conditions on border trade was also made apparent by another incident associated with the ouster of former prime minister Khin Nyunt, which occurred on October 19, 2004, when I was in Mae Sot. I heard the news from an NGO worker that evening, and the next day, the Burmese in Mae Sot were excitedly talking about the incident. Local Thais also offered their political analyses. At that time, Prime Minister Thaksin, who was in Mae Sot on October 19, 2004, canceled his plan to visit Myawaddy and headed back to Bangkok (Bangkok Post 2004a). NGOs in Mae Sot held emergency meetings and calculated the foreseeable outcomes concerning the refugees. Allegedly, one of the reasons for the ousting of the prime minister was his implication in corruption (Nation 2004). He and many of his staff and aides were arrested and taken into custody at the Thailand-Myanmar border and the China-Myanmar border (Bangkok Post 2004b; 2004c). The removal of Khin Nyunt influenced, in particular, the volume of exports from Mae Sot.

<Table 3> Volumes of Exports and Imports from July 2004 to November 2004 through the Mae Sot Customs Office (Unit: 1 million baht)

Month/Year	Exports	Imports
Jul. 2004	1,053	47
Aug. 2004	1,165	69
Sep. 2004	1,121	61
Oct. 2004	862	63
Nov. 2004	843	58

Source: Mae Sot Customs Office

Before this incident, the export volume had stabilized at more than 1 billion baht. However, in October and November of 2004, the volume suddenly decreased, most likely owing to the unstable political situation in Myanmar. Compared to the export volume, the import volume does not clearly show the effect of Khin Nyunt's arrest. This difference demonstrates that political conditions than imports more directly influence exports from Thailand to Myanmar.

It also shows that importation occurs largely informally and autonomously.

All of this provides evidence that changes in political environments influence the dynamics of border trade and that traders thus devise adaptation strategies, oscillating between the bridge and the boat. Different political and legal situations in the two neighboring countries accelerate the magnitude of cross-border movements, where the legal/formal and the illegal/informal intersect.

The Ordering of the Border

An understanding of unofficial border-crossing by boat cannot be complete without taking into account the ethnic politics that constitute the ordering of the border. As shown earlier, when the black markets were active, the KNU was responsible for them without the state's involvement. However, another group, the DKBA (Democratic Karen Buddhist Army), has now replaced the KNU in cooperating with the Myanmar government. Although the Myanmar government appears to control the border on the Myanmar side, it cannot exercise a full scale of governance. One strategy adopted by the Myanmar government in order to target this problem has been to provide a "carrot" for ethnic groups and to turn them into border guards under the government's control—the carrot being a license for border trade. Hence, ethnic groups were allowed to control the movement of goods and relevant taxes (Bangkok Post 2004d). On the Myawaddy side of the border, the government collaborated with the DKBA (Lintner 1999: 297). In return, the DKBA was allowed to control the border-crossing points along the river and extract some revenue by taxing goods and people. Among the points controlled, the nearest is located just several minutes away on foot from the bridge. According to Burmese informants, people crossing the Moei River through the piers had to pay around five hundred kyat in the mid-2000s. In addition to the movement of people, many imported and exported goods were taxed when passing through these points.

The Myanmar government has exploited the split of the Karen and associated with the DKBA for its border control. A patron-client relationship between the DKBA and the Myanmar government was initiated and strengthened under former prime minister Khin Nyunt (August 2003-October 2004). When Khin Nyunt was in power, the DKBA enjoyed substantial economic gains from shipping and distributing Japanese used cars through its crossing points along the border. The scale of the cross-border movement of cars was enormous. Many local traders testified that hundreds of cars passed through the Moei River by boat during the heyday of this trade. The Three Pagoda Pass also served as a significant entry point for cars into Myanmar. The DKBA was the exclusively dominant player in the used car business. Burmese traders and individual buyers had to apply to the group to make a transaction. La Poh, one of my informants from Mawlamyine, admitted, on June 21, 2005, that while she worked in the car business in Mawlamyine and the Three Pagoda Pass, it was impossible to run such a business without the permission of the DKBA.

However, the ouster of Khin Nyunt made a significant impact on border trade and, in particular, on the DKBA. The group lost its business opportunities, notably the transportation of Japanese used cars, which the ousted Khin Nyunt had granted. The familiar scene of cars passing through the DKBA checkpoints became obsolete after this period, and the group's revenue from border trade decreased sharply.

Despite the removal of Khin Nyunt, the DKBA continued its strong collaboration with the Myanmar government. The government placed the group more closely under its umbrella, pushing to use the collaborative ethnic groups scattered along the border for state border guards. As a result of this move, the DKBA became the guard in charge of the border with neighboring Thailand. The official status transformation ceremony took place on August 18, 2010 (Democratic Voice of Burma 2012). However, this move became a source of internal conflict within the group: one section, DKBA Brigade 5, refused to be incorporated into the force because the status change meant a loss of control of their weapons and autonomy. In the end, the dissident group attacked a government military camp in Myawaddy on November 8, 2010, and a battle ensued. This incident prompted the exodus of hundreds of civilians from Myawaddy to Mae Sot (Bangkok Post 2010). The conflicts were later settled, and the DKBA has continued to serve as a border guard force, although the dissident section has not joined (Democratic Voice of Burma 2012).[51]

Local Thai exporters knew who was in charge of the flow of goods. Border traders negotiate the political reality in a highly

51 The dissident faction formed the Democratic Karen Benevolent Army on November 8, 2010 while the original DKBA became the Border Guard Force. See http://www.mmpeacemonitor.org/stakeholders/myanmar-peace-center/159-dkba-5 (accessed October 15, 2014). This name change causes some confusion since now the DKBA refers to the Democratic Karen Benevolent Group. However, I refer to the original group as the DKBA since it also covers the story prior to the group's split.

pragmatic way to keep operating their businesses (Schoenberger and Turner 2008: 667-696). Their ability to access the border comes from local knowledge of political environments accumulated over many years. In particular, they know precisely to which border point they should send their goods, and they use several processes to move their goods across the border. My informant, Ekamon, a textile trader, is contacted by phone by his customer in Yangon, who places an order for items. Ekamon takes the ordered items in his truck to the border. After going through the Mae Sot customs office, they are brought to a Thai-side boat pier, where Burmese workers load them onto a boat. They are then taken to a DKBA checkpoint on the Myawaddy side. The imported items are taxed by the DKBA and afterward transported into Myanmar by vehicle. Local Thai exporters somehow consider the DKBA as a business partner without whom border trade would be impossible. This portrayal problematizes the conventional image of the DKBA, which is often depicted as an immoral armed band that destabilizes the border. Like it or not, the group has become an indispensable player in keeping trade active at the border.

The DKBA acts as a partner, even for the Mae Sot customs office, which cannot avoid interactions with the group and thus considers that the DKBA's involvement in border trade is routine. The warehouses established by the office did not appear to operate well without collaboration from the DKBA. For efficient and optimal operation, it was necessary to have similar warehouse capacities on the other side of the border. It shows that the international ordering of the border is not necessarily associated with government-to-government relations. Often a state agency on one side deals with a non-state agency on the other side during cross-border communication. The story of the DKBA thus demonstrates how internal and international orders work along the border.

Conclusion

In this chapter, I have portrayed the behind-the-scenes informal economic activities in the Thailand-Myanmar borderland. As critical factors that facilitate this informality, I have pointed out people's intimacy with the borderland, commodity exchanges that take on local consumption patterns, and the ethnic networks that mediate the movement of goods. Local traders are never marginal but active players, employing their local knowledge and mobility deep-rooted in the border, overcoming state regulatory practices, and navigating the formal-informal intersection. The exported and imported commodities practically validate the presence of local traders so that they can meet the needs of people across the border, even though the scale and mode of the cross-border commodity exchange may take different shapes depending on political and economic conditions. In particular, ethnic groups play an essential role in moving goods across the border in cooperation with local traders and state agencies. The order of the border has emerged from this collaboration among various actors.

The cases addressed here challenge the social marginality approach of the informal border trade and economy, which tends to describe it as marginal, pathological, and hence disconnected from the formal economy. This chapter has demonstrated, along with the state regulation or integration approach, that the division between the formal/legal and the informal/illegal is often situational and arbitrary. In practice, the two domains intersect, as evidenced by the cross-border movement of goods, wherein different legal standards apply on each side of the border. This nexus is inevitable, given that ontologically, the two domains are always intrinsic to each other in that order creates disorder, and the formal creates the informal (Lomnitz 1988: 54; Portes and Haller 2005: 409). This integration scope prompts us to adopt an alternative distinction between the licit—what is socially acceptable—and the illicit—what is otherwise—as Abraham and van Schendel (2005) suggest. While this chapter has demonstrated that smuggling epitomizes the illegal but licit, it has also shed more light on how people mobilize their cultural resources and local networks to overcome regulations and navigate this nexus, thus building upon the small firms approach.

The formal and informal nexus has its own dynamics as different social groups compete to appropriate the border for symbolic or practical purposes. For the state, it is a symbolic marker of state sovereignty, whereas, for the borderlanders, it is a living space. The borderlanders' cognitive map, as drawn from their daily lives, does not correspond to the statist scale that regulates the limit and mode of the movement of people and goods (Van Schendel 2005a: 55-56; 2005b: 375-377). This scaling difference often causes tension and conflict between different parties. State regulations to enforce the spatial scale on the border, as evidenced by the wall-building initiative along the riverbank, are often transgressed and appropriated by the borderlanders to their advantage. The locals counteract the state's ordering practices by employing their local knowledge and mobility, on the one hand, while profoundly rooting themselves in the terrain of the borderland, on the other hand. In these encounters, the border is reimagined, negotiated, and redrawn.

However, at the same time, as Donnan and Wilson (1999: 88) note, the merchants are seldom revolutionary. Their existence, in some sense, depends on the state—in particular, the border that the state seeks to establish. Their livelihood relies on the differences in the goods and prices the border brings about. Similarly, the state also relies on informality or illegality in their statecraft because illegality often provides a clue with which the state can enhance its ordering capacity (Soguk 1999). The presence of illegality does not necessarily weaken the state; instead, it ultimately empowers it. Moreover, as observed in the illustration of the ethnic groups in this chapter, the state counts on non-state authorities to operate border trade and to protect the border. Informality and formality are complementary. All of these factors challenge the formal and informal dichotomy, requiring us to recognize the intersecting dynamics of the situation.

This chapter has implications for the cross-border development of the region and beyond, given that border towns are being appropriated as nodes in regional cross-border integration processes and global supply chains. The building of a second Thai-Myanmar Friendship Bridge that had been under discussion by the governments of Thailand and Myanmar during my stay became complete. It was officially opened to traffic on October 30, 2019 (Thai PBS World 2019). This project represents the anticipation that the governments and transnational capital will facilitate border trade and develop border towns as pivotal gateways for advancing to neighboring countries and beyond, as evidenced in the case of the fourth Thai-Lao Friendship Bridge (Lin and Grundy-Warr 2012). The second Thai-Myanmar Friendship Bridge is expected, likewise, to become pivotal as a transnational link. In addition, the plan to develop Mae Sot into a special economic zone reflects the state's and capital's endeavors to position the border town as a strategic hub of trade and industry (Bangkok Post 2014b; Campbell 2018; Swe and Chambers 2011). The democratization of Myanmar (2010-2021) indeed brought more opportunities for Mae Sot. It is part of the significant regional transformation underway in the GMS. Regional connectivity will bring more capital, laborers, and traders to the border towns and the existing layers (Arnold and Hewison 2005: 335-33; Phianphachong 2018).

The future state of unauthorized trade, now conducted behind the scenes as *withi chiwit*, will unfold further in this regional context. Local traders will have to navigate their pursuit of *withi chiwit* through regional integration processes. It is important to note that their mobility and sense of space, as developed over the years, will likely provide a strong foundation for their future navigation of *withi chiwit*, which would undoubtedly play out in a more dynamic setting.

Chapter 5

Migrant Schools: From the Informal to the Formal

Introduction

This chapter investigates how a non-state educational institution has emerged and how it came to get a certain level of state recognition. In seeking this objective, I put a central focus on the roles of agencies such as migrant leaders, NGOs, and state educational agencies and relations among them because the building of the migrant educational institution came into being as a result of the involvement and collaborations of these agencies.

Since 1991, when the first migrant school opened with a few enrolled students, the number of migrant schools and enrolled students has dramatically increased. In particular, the latter part of the 2000s saw a massive expansion. In 2010, 61 migrant schools accommodated over 11,000 migrant students in the town and its adjacent areas (Migrant Educational Co-ordination Center 2010). As of the early 2020s, the schools continued to run in a similar capacity.[52] It means that a "migrant institution" has emerged, firmly and visibly rooted in almost every migrant living compound scattered throughout the town.

In the middle of the 2000s, migrant schools faced a turning point: eventually, the Thai government became involved in migrant education. The government's key intention was to turn them into regular learning centers under its guidance. This move brought migrant schools into an unprecedented phase. Despite the controversy, migrant schools were in the process of transferring from informal to formal.

Conventional approaches to the study of minority/migration

52 https://www.mecctak2.com/, accessed December 9, 2022.

education have mainly focused on how minority students adapt to the educational environments of the host countries (Eldering et al. 1989; Gibson 1985; Hien 1999; Suárez-Orozco and Suárez-Orozco 2001). These approaches examined the performance of migrant children in the educational settings of the host societies. In explaining the differences in academic performances among migrant children, scholars analyzed various factors affecting students' achievements. Some scholars investigated cultural differences between origins and host societies, including language and customs (Erickson 1984; Lein 1975; Ogbu 1982). Others pointed out structural constraints and attributed the low achievement of migrant students to the system of social stratification where minority students take low positions (Aronowitz and Giroux and 1993; MacLeod 1995; Orfield 1998). Schools function to allocate themselves such positions that the social structure may be reproduced (Bourdieu and Passeron 1990). However, one thread of study examined how minority students manage to overcome structural constraints and make use of education in the host societies as a strategy for upward social mobility in host societies (Moldenhawer 2005; Westin 2003).

Performance differences among migrant students in given structural settings led some scholars to develop a cultural-ecological model (Gibson and Ogbu 1991; Ogbu 1989; 1991; Weis 1990). This model distinguishes between voluntary and involuntary minorities and suggests that the former positively react to the schooling of the host societies and achieve higher performance. In contrast, the latter are unlikely to study hard because they do not wish to assimilate into the host societies and see that schooling does not benefit them much in already cast-like stratified societies (Conchas 2001: 477). All in all, scholars' interest in the school performance of migrant students focused attention on the educational methods that help the students adapt to the schooling of the host societies. Here many methods, including bilingual teaching, mobile education, curriculum change, and parental involvement, have been introduced (Carreon et al. 2005; Fisher et al. 2002; Leon 1996; López et al. 2001)

Migrant education in Mae Sot sharply differs from the cases of existing research in that the migrant students in the town pursue an educational opportunity in migrant schools set up by migrant leaders together with NGOs, not in the formal schools of the host society. They do not necessarily need to adapt or conform to the education system of the host society. Migrant education as a quasi-regular form of education system substantially operates alongside the Thai education system in the town.

Of course, the education of migrant children in the setting of migrant schools is not a rare case. Other countries have similar cases. For instance, the US-Mexico borderland, European countries, Nigeria, and China have similar schools for migrant children, as already explored in the discussion of migrant enclaves (Fong and Murphy 2006; Gobbo 2009; Macias 1996; Umar and Tahir 2009; Van Daele and van Poucke 1984; Weiler 1994). However, these migrant schools were mainly set up by the state as government schools. Most migrant students are internal citizens in the cases of Nigeria and China. In contrast, migrant schools in Mae Sot were established by Burmese migrants themselves in cooperation with NGOs, and enrolled migrant students are foreign nationals.

Hence, the critical issues of migrant education in Mae Sot do not remain in adaptation to and academic performance in the schools of the host society, as has been considered by existing research thus far. Instead, with an expanded scope, we should relate migrant schools to the lives of migrants in general. Here I attempt to approach them by focusing on institutional building. The establishment of migrant schools marked a turning point in the pattern of migrants' settlement in Mae Sot. It means that the pattern became more institutionalized and stabilized in an institutional base by establishing the schools compared to the past when they lacked a firm foundation.

In conventional understanding, establishing institutions is often linked with recognition and authorization from the state or other authorized parties. In other words, institutions are closely associated with formalization and legalization. However, institution-building in migrant education in Mae Sot was not based on legal and formal structures. Initially, it did not adhere to the state's laws and regulations. Although informal and illegal, migrant schools in Mae Sot operated constantly and regularly, i.e., as a "non-state informal institution." Part of understanding why it became possible concerns the societal formation of the border town. Undocumented migrants are already crucial components in sustaining the border town's social system, and informality is not an abnormal feature but a legitimate one in its standard. While the central power's influence has been limited in the area, a non-state institution has grown relatively easily. It shows that any understanding of migrant education must come with the social and political conditions in a particular place where migrant schools exist.

My association with migrant education entails some elaborative explanation of my engagement. Among the migrant schools, my focus school was Hsa Thoo Lei School. The school played a central role in mobilizing activities across the schools and was a primary contact point for government education agencies and NGOs. Also, my focus group was the teachers in the school since the headmaster was the chairperson of an umbrella organization of migrant schools, the Burmese Migrant Workers' Education Committee (BMWEC). Thus by closely associating with the school, I was able to understand how migrant schools operated in general, as well as how concerned parties engaged in migrant education.

To gather information on the government's policy, I visited the local educational agency of the government, the Education Service Area Office (ESAO) 2 of Tak Province, which is in charge of education matters in the western districts of the Province.[53] Through the visits to the office, I got the complete version of the information on migrant schools, including the number of schools, students, teachers, establishment years, and curriculum. For the ethnographic observation of the state's engagement, I participated in a gathering organized by the ESAO 2 to explain the government's policy to school leaders and NGOs.

Lastly, I also visited educational NGOs. The leading NGO, World Education/Consortium (WE/C), was my crucial informant organization. Through unstructured and structured interviews with the NGO, I was able to investigate how NGOs are involved in migrant education, and they react to the government's intervention.

The Development of Migrant Schools

As Figure 1 indicates, in the 1990s, the number of migrant schools

53 The ESAO 1 covers the eastern part of Tak Province.

remained low. However, stepping into 2000, the number jumped and increased yearly throughout the 2000s. Why did the number of migrant schools suddenly increase in the 2000s compared to the 1990s?

<Figure 1> The Growth of Migrant Schools

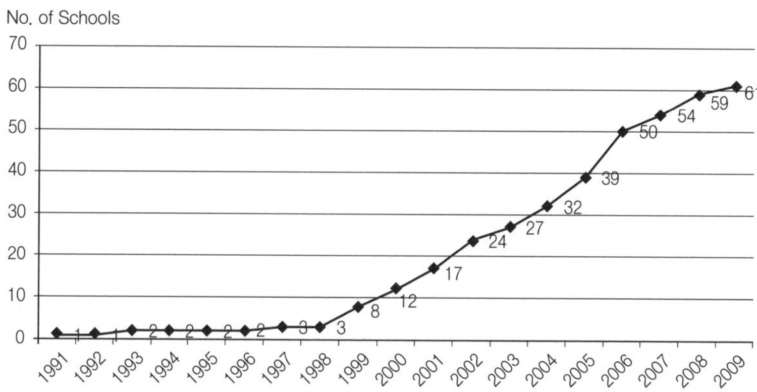

Source: Migrant Educational Co-ordination Center 2010

In the 1990s, the establishment and operation of migrant schools were mainly the outcomes of migrant individuals' endeavors and the support from individual foreigners. However, migrant leaders realized the importance of collaborating, and finally, they organized a collective form, the Burmese Migrant Workers' Education Committee, to promote education for migrant children in 1999. Once organized, it played a significant role in mobilizing resources to establish migrant schools and cooperating with international partners. Meanwhile, NGOs, which had used to focus on activities inside refugee camps, began to sense that undocumented migrants in the town areas also needed humanitarian support and consequently focused on them. In this combination of the collective endeavors of migrant leaders in the form of BMWEC and NGOs' involvement in the causes of migrants, a new chapter of the history of migrant education took off.

The growth of migrant schools, of course, expanded the number of enrolled students. The growth trend of student enrollment followed a similar pattern to that of migrant school numbers. As shown below, in the 1990s, only a handful of migrant children attended migrant schools. However, the number shot up, passing through the 2000s.

<Figure 2> Total Student Enrollment by School Year

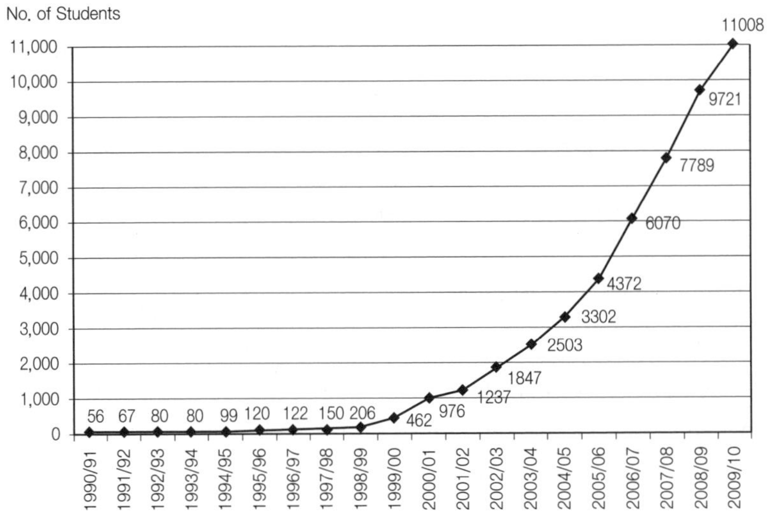

Source: Migrant Educational Co-ordination Center 2010

What is conspicuous in migrant schools is that English takes the most considerable portion in curriculum formation. It is related to the specific conditions of the town where international organizations and foreign individuals constitute a prominent position in educational matters as well as in many other sectors of society, such as labor and democratic activities. Here, English draws much attention due to the migrants' attempts to communicate effectively with foreigners. It displays how Burmese leaders practically approach education to survive in a vulnerable situation and keep pace with the changing world. For them, education carries not just pedagogical purpose but also survival means.

Curriculum

In the Burmese national education system, students receive eleven years of education from primary to secondary or high school. Primary education comprises KG[54] to Grade Four; middle school comprises Grades Five to Eight; high school comprises Grades Nine to Ten. The migrant schools in Mae Sot also follow this structure. Depending on space and available teachers, the levels they offered were different. Thus, migrant students in certain schools who want to further their education must transfer to other schools.

According to the Boarding Middle School for Orphans and Helpless Youths (BMSOH) School, which had a total of seventy-four students, only twenty-four were enrolled in Grades Five to Eight. It means that the enrollment rate of secondary-level students is relatively low. A reason for this could be the inadequacy of existing school facilities and human resources. However, this reason might not be compelling as there were many qualified teachers holding university degrees capable of teaching at the high school level. Another reason could be that the absolute number of secondary-

54 Usually the KG (kindergarten) grade offers one-year education. However, those who are not qualified to enter the first grade need to study two years at the KG level.

level students is small. However, one often encounters many of these teenagers in and around Mae Sot who are not attending high school education. Therefore, the most probable reason would be that most teenagers of this age group work in the town and its vicinity to support their families instead of pursuing higher education. Especially since the fulfillment of education in migrant schools does not guarantee entry into the Thai job market, these teenagers lose interest in continuing their education in migrant schools.

The Karen Youth Leadership and Management Training Center (KYLMTC) offers the post-Tenth grade program. Most students are Karen from refugee camps and Karen State. They seek accommodation in the school. The subjects taught in the school include English, social studies, history, computer literacy, and management studies. Some foreigners also take up teaching positions voluntarily for three months.

In terms of textbooks, standard Burmese school textbooks are used in teaching. However, Karen migrant schools and Elpis Center use refugee camp textbooks, whereas Muslim migrant schools incorporate Arabic and religious subjects into their curriculum.

Subjects offered in BMSOH are as follows: at the primary school level, basic English literature, basic arithmetic, Burmese, geography, and basic general science; and at middle and high school level, English language and basic grammar, arithmetic, algebra, geometry, Burmese, geography, and general science. In the case of Hsa Thoo Lei School, a Karen school, the subjects taught include Burmese, Karen, Thai, English, mathematics, geography, sciences, history, and sewing and handicraft. The inclusion of the Karen language is conspicuous in the composition of the curriculum, compared to non-

Karen migrant schools. The school uses Burmese national textbooks at the primary level and refugee camp textbooks at the secondary level. Life Page School offers English, Burmese, Thai, mathematics, social sciences, history, sciences, Burmese culture, art and music, and sewing and handicraft. In the case of a Muslim school, Arabic, Thai, English, Burmese, mathematics, and sciences are offered. Most migrant schools teach Thai, though inconsistent. Thai Karen or local Thai individuals take the job of teaching Thai.

In terms of timetable, the case of the Children's Development Center (CDC) is shown in Table 4.

<Table 4> Timetable of the CDC Migrant School

KG

Mon	English	English	Science	Burmese	Break	Thai	Math	Math
Tue	English	English	Science	Burmese	Break	Thai	Math	Math
Wed	English	English	Science	Burmese	Break	Thai	Math	Math
Thu	English	Burmese	Science	Burmese	Break	Thai	Thai	Math
Fri	English	Burmese	Science	Burmese	Break	Special Activities		

First Standard

Mon	Burmese	Burmese	Science	Thai	Break	Math	English	English
Tue	Burmese	Burmese	Science	Thai	Break	Math	English	English
Wed	Burmese	Math	Science	Thai	Break	Math	English	English
Thu	Burmese	Math	Science	Thai	Break	Math	English	English
Fri	Burmese	Math	Science	Thai	Break	Special Activities		

Second Standard

Mon	Burmese	Burmese	English	Math	Break	English	Thai	Science
Tue	Burmese	Burmese	English	Math	Break	English	Thai	Science
Wed	Burmese	Thai	English	Math	Break	Math	Thai	Science
Thu	Burmese	English	English	Math	Break	Math	Thai	Science
Fri	Burmese	English	Science	Math	Break	Special Activities		

Third Standard

Mon	Math	Math	Thai	G/H*	Break	English	G/H	Burmese
Tue	Math	Math	Thai	English	Break	G/H	Science	Burmese
Wed	Math	Science	Thai	G/H	Break	Burmese	English	Thai
Thu	Math	Science	Thai	English	Break	G/H	Burmese	Burmese
Fri	Math	Science	English	English	Break	Special Activities		

* Geography/History

Fourth Standard

Mon	English	English	Thai	Burmese	Break	Science	Math	G/H
Tue	English	Thai	Math	Burmese	Break	Science	Math	G/H
Wed	English	English	Science	Burmese	Break	Thai	Burmese	G/H
Thu	English	English	Science	Math	Break	Math	Thai	G/H
Fri	English	Math	Math	Burmese	Break	Special Activities		

Fifth Standard

Mon	Science	Math	Math	Math	Break	English	English	Thai
Tue	Science	Math	Burmese	G/H	Break	English	English	Thai
Wed	Science	Math	Burmese	G/H	Break	English	Computer	Thai
Thu	Science	Math	Burmese	G/H	Break	English	Computer	Thai
Fri	Science	Burmese	Math	G/H	Break	Special Activities		

Sixth Standard

Mon	Thai	English	English	Science	Break	Math	Burmese	Math
Tue	Thai	English	G/H	Science	Break	Math	Burmese	Math
Wed	Thai	English	G/H	Science	Break	Computer	Burmese	Math
Thu	Thai	English	G/H	Science	Break	Computer	Burmese	Math
Fri	English	G/H	G/H	Science	Break	Special Activities		

The example of the CDC should not be taken as a model for all migrant schools because it is relatively well-organized. Under the management of Dr. Cynthia and the Mae Tao Clinic, it has adequate teachers and enjoys relatively good facilities and funding. Other schools, tiny ones, face difficulties keeping to the timetable due to a shortage of teachers and study rooms for each level. Thus, it was not rare that teachers ran a combined class comprising students of different levels.

Nevertheless, the timetable of the CDC provides a general picture of subjects taught in migrant schools. As we can see from the table above, students from all levels have thirty-two hours of learning per week, except for special activities on Friday afternoons. Students study for four hours before lunch, after which they continue for three hours.

Concerning curriculum composition, Burmese, English, Thai, Math, and Science are taught in all grades, whereas Geography and History are added from the third grade onwards. Computer lessons are offered from the fifth grade. It is notable that from the kindergarten level, migrant children are required to learn three languages - Burmese, Thai, and English - which could be a burden for them. English takes up the most significant component of teaching hours, as shown in Table 5.

<Table 5> Teaching Hours of Subjects (Weekly)

Subject	KG	First Standard	Second Standard	Third Standard	Fourth Standard	Fifth Standard	Sixth Standard	Total
English	8	8	8	6	8	6	6	50
Burmese	7	7	7	5	5	4	4	39
Thai	5	5	5	5	4	4	4	32
Math	7	7	7	7	7	7	6	48
Science	5	5	5	4	4	5	5	33
G/H				5	4	4	5	18
Computer						2	2	4

The emphasis on language education, especially English, is not specific to the CDC. Other migrant schools also place more emphasis on English than other subjects. It is not unrelated to the specific conditions of the town, where international organizations and foreign individuals constitute a prominent position in educational matters as well as in many other sectors of society, such as labor and democratic activities. According to one of my informants and from my observation, Mae Sot might rank first regarding the number of foreigners per capita in Thailand. Migrant leaders encounter them daily. Here, English draws much attention due to the migrants' attempts to communicate effectively with foreigners. Many migrant activists and refugee leaders revealed that the most apparent difference observed since they came to Mae Sot was the cooperation with international parties and individuals. It was reflected in the running of the migrant schools. The bias toward teaching English over other subjects was deplorable for some people. My informant in an Educational NGO lamented, "English is not a medium of education anymore but becomes all about education here." However, many Burmese leaders regarded it as a means of survival in a vulnerable situation and keeping pace with the changing world. In some measure, it shows how less-privileged people confront their difficulties through education. Including Thai in the curriculum also demonstrates this coping strategy in Thai society.

Connections with Partners

Relationships with Refugee Camps

Due to geographical proximity and human flow between Mae

Sot and the refugee camps, migrant schools have had intimate relations with refugee schools. In comparison, the refugee education system runs more systematically and in a more organized manner than the migrant education system does because the Karen have a long history of running their education system, which has been maintained in the refugee camps despite the engagement of educational NGOs. Furthermore, refugee camps' confinement is a conductive factor for refugee leaders to mobilize refugee students to attend camp schools. Above all, the Karen Education Department (KED) role of the Karen National Union has been prominent from the beginning. Almost every school in Karen refugee camps follows the regulations and directions of the KED.

In contrast, migrant education, despite the progress over the years, has not yet achieved such a standard. At first, refugee education was a model for migrant schools. Many migrant schools adopted textbooks used in refugee schools and operational styles such as teachers' training systems. Even they were provided with refugee teachers to start migrant education. The connection between the two school types is prominent, in particular, in Karen migrant schools. It is not because they lack capacity as compared to other migrant schools but because they have more intimate relationships with refugee camps which stems from their ethnic affinity. The KED was involved in Karen migrant schools such as Hsa Thoo Lei School. The school was primarily indebted to refugee schools. Ironically, refugee camps, commonly regarded as backward and abandoned areas, have become a model to emulate.

Collaborations between the two sectors can also occur in student exchanges. Many refugee students visited migrant schools and presented cultural performances. In turn, migrant students who graduated from high school with good academic performance were sent to refugee camps to pursue higher-level education at the Further Studies Program and bible schools there. Migrant schools are often used as transit education for refugee children who resided in the town for specific purposes. The town and refugee camps are education-linked (Lee 2012).

The role of NGOs is influential in this connectivity. NGOs that used to do relief activities for refugees have now turned to migrant education, and their experiences in refugee education are thus translated into implementing migrant education. My finding revealed that three NGOs-WE/C, the International Rescue Committee (IRC), and the Jesuit Refugee Service (JRS)-which used to be involved in refugee education began migrant education. Other NGOs, such as ZOA (Zuidoost-Azië)[55] Refugee Care, for example, decided to expand their operations to the migrants. Among the NGOs named above, IRC and JRS offered financial support to migrant schools, whereas WE/C worked on creating a standard curriculum and teacher training programs.[56] In 2004/05, I observed that the NGOs experienced difficulties engaging in migrant education mainly because of their unfamiliarity. They struggled to determine the direction for migrant education. They encountered some practical problems, such as using the Burmese language in daily activities, with which local NGO workers, mainly Karen, were unfamiliar. Above all, they had to deal with many stakeholders, such as migrant school leaders and Thai authorities, compared to the case of refugee

55 This Dutch word means "Southeast Asia."

56 Interview with a migrant education team leader of the WE/C (April 26, 2005).

education, where they only dealt with the KED. Nevertheless, educational NGOs were determined to improve migrant education since they felt it imperative for migrant children who had been neglected for a long time. NGO donors became interested in migrant education and started funding it (Kraft 2004). From the late 2000s, the involvement of NGOs seemed to achieve positive outcomes with the instigation of a standard curriculum and the strengthening and increased stability of the collaboration with migrant leaders.

Collaborations with International Partners

Many foreign organizations and individuals are directly or indirectly involved in migrant education. For instance, the teacher wages of Hsa Thoo Lei School came from the Federation of Trade Unions Burma, food from the Burma Refugee Care Program, and computers and student stationeries from individual foreigners and organizations. Children's Dream played a central role in constructing the Hsa Thoo Lei School building and the extension of the learning center in the CDC.[57] Besides material support, many international parties and individuals participate in other areas, such as administrative matters and the training of teachers.

One critical issue related to international partners is the absence of a coordinating body. It also contrasts with the coordinating body of refugee relief NGOs. In the case of relief assistance for refugees, they shared project information and coordinated their activities through monthly meetings to avoid duplication and neglect under the direction of an umbrella organization, the

57 For details, see the website of Children's Dream (http://www.childrensdream.org).

Committee for Coordination of Services to Displaced Persons in Thailand (CCSDPT), which was formed in 1975. In contrast, migrant education has not yet achieved this level of cooperation and coordination, partly because, compared with refugee camps, organizations and individuals engaging in migrant education do not have entry restrictions into Mae Sot. It is relatively easy for them to begin relief activities without state recognition and endorsement. This continuous in-flow of external actors has made it challenging to regularize and coordinate the activities of international partners. However, the absence of the coordinating body of NGOs, in turn, has strengthened the role of BMWEC, which became a governing body and played a coordinating role. It shows that at least the nominal representative of migrant schools is in the hands of the migrants themselves. BMWEC's representative role is not restricted to the border but extends to international areas. For example, it participated in international gatherings such as the Asia Pacific Consultation on Refugee Rights, ASEAN People Forum and Regional Conference on Migration (BMWEC 2009: 8).

Connections with Thai locals

As shown earlier, Thai locals play some role in migrant schools. Directly or indirectly, many Thai locals contributed to the migrant schools. For example, a Thai Karen rented out the compound of Hsa Thoo Lei School, a Thai mosque accommodated a migrant school, and a local Thai church cooperated with Elpis.

However, not all Thai locals have positive attitudes toward migrant schools. They often complained about the noise pollution and disease-spreading potential of migrant schools in their neighborhood. However, indeed, very few local Thais were disturbed by migrant schools. Most migrant schools are located within migrant living compounds, seldom accommodating Thai locals, and interference with the locals rarely occurs. Indeed the migrants benefit them, providing cheap labor and purchasing goods from the stores of local people.

Thai locals gained educational benefits as well as these economic benefits. For example, Hsa Thoo Lei School sent their English and Burmese language teachers to a nearby Thai school. For the Thai school, it was incredibly beneficial to learn Burmese and English from native speakers. A migrant school in a mosque accommodated Thai students on weekends, where they studied Burmese and English. In exchange for allowing the school's operations within the mosque, it needed to take care of some Thai students. For Thai students, Burmese and English languages are essential. Notably, many Thai locals wanted to learn Burmese to attend to Burmese customers better and find investment opportunities in Burma. Migrant schools, for them, are learning places to meet their practical needs. These examples demonstrate that the presence of migrant schools benefits not just the Burmese migrants but the Thai locals.

Some local Thai schools actively promote collaboration with migrant schools on a regular base. For instance, Ban Tha Art School, located near the Burmese border, signed a memorandum of understanding with five migrant schools to provide them with Thai language classes (Bangkok Post 2009). Local Thai education parties actively promote this collaboration trend (Migrant Educational Co-ordination Center 2010: 16).

Migrant students were open to activities of the Thai schools.

For example, three students of a school run by the Burma Labour Solidarity Organization (BLSO) were the winners of a province-wide poetry reading and public speaking competition where students read and spoke in Thai, competing against other students in their age group. It was an outstanding achievement for them to win the prize, competing with native Thai speakers (BLSO 2006: 1). Although interactions between migrant schools and Thai schools do not occur extensively, the former is gaining greater recognition from the latter as partners.

The State and Migrant Schools

State's Regulatory Actions

Regarding migrant education, the state used to be indifferent to managing education in migrant schools. However, in 2004/5, the state began to show a positive attitude toward migrant schools, approaching migrant schools with a seemingly pure educational purpose. Mainly initiated by the monarchy, in particular Princess Maha Chakri Sirindhorn, migrant education attracted attention under the slogan of "Education for All,"[58] where all children, regardless of legal status, should be offered basic education without barriers to a certain level.[59]

58 The movement of Education for All is a global movement initiated and coordinated by the United Nations Educational, Scientific and Cultural Organization (UNESCO). For further details, refer to the website (http://www.unesco.org/education/efa/ed_for_all/, accessed October 24, 2011).

59 Princess Maha Chakri Sirindhorn's approaches to education for migrant people can be found in Bangkok Post (2002).

The monarchy's keen interest in migrant education prompted the Ministry of Education (MOE) to develop education policies for migrants and refugees. In January 2005, MOE launched a survey on migrant education. MOE officials began to visit Mae Sot and organized meetings with migrant education leaders and education NGOs such as WE/C and ZOA Refugee Care. Despite their illegal residence in Mae Sot, migrant leaders were invited or requested to join the meetings. Migrant education leaders presented on migrant schools in Mae Sot and its adjacent areas, mentioning the problems and suggestions about migrant education before the government officials. The government officials also explained the government's plans for migrant children.

In the end, MOE came up with policies for migrant education, and on July 5, 2005, a Cabinet Resolution on the education of undocumented and non-Thai persons was passed. The critical point of the resolution is that the government offers all migrant children, regardless of legality, education from kindergarten up to high school. In doing this, the resolution mentions that the budget for the education of non-Thai students will be at the same rate as Thai students. The students will be issued with a 13-digit personal identity number and given travel passes to allow them to travel to school (Asian Migrant Centre 2005: 122; Office of the Educational Council of MOE 2008).

After the resolution, MOE continued developing subsequent policies and plans. Its significant move was to register migrant schools as "Learning Centers" and incorporate them into the state education system. In consultation with migrant schools and international organizations, MOE has set forth some guidelines on the steps that migrant schools need to follow under the directions or jurisdiction of MOE (Guinard 2006:8; Irrawaddy 2006c). One of the requirements for them was to include the teaching of Thai.

Although the government showed an active involvement in migrant education in 2005, continuous political turmoil, including the military coup in September 2006 and frequent changes in the government formation in the latter part of the 2000s, hindered the education agency from achieving these initial goals. Finally, the government introduced a detailed plan by drafting the "Regulation of the Office of the Prime Minister on Educational Provision for Individuals with No Civil Registration or No Thai Nationality by Non-Governmental Organizations in Migrant Learning Centers" in June 2009. This plan was discussed at a meeting held in Mae Sot on June 23-24, 2009 between MOE officials, migrant education leaders, and concerned NGOs. The drafted regulation stipulates the formation and roles of a national committee. The committee's primary responsibility is to set policies and directions for the educational provision of migrant learning resources and migrant learning centers.

The regulation further stipulates the implementing body of the policies at the local level. The Education Service Area Office (ESAO) of the Provinces where migrant learning centers are located shall have a local-level committee consisting of the governor or an entrusted person as chairperson and not more than ten representatives of related agencies in the areas appointed by the governor. The director of the ESAO shall be the secretary of the local committee, and a deputy director and a staff member of the ESAO shall become assistant secretaries of the local committee. For migrant education leaders and NGOs, the ESAO is the most immediate partner. In the case of migrant schools in Mae Sot, it is the ESAO 2 of Tak Province. Indeed, ESAO 2 has been actively involved in migrant schools. It established the Migrant Educational Co-ordination Center in 2008 to coordinate with migrant leaders and NGOs and regularly met with them at least every other month (Migrant Educational Co-ordination Center 2010: 11).

The regulation also regularizes the process of establishing a migrant learning center. For instance, the founder of it has to submit a request for permission containing the details such as education levels, curriculum, and the names of teachers. The curriculum section included in the drafted regulation clearly describes the inclusion of an understanding of Thai society and language.

The regulation demonstrates that the state is attempting to regulate migrant schools under its strict guidelines. I observed this at a meeting where the ESAO 2 instructed migrant schools to follow the guideline on January 14, 2010. The director of the ESAO 2 at the meeting stated,

> I believe that you think that you and your children will have to continue to stay in Thailand. Therefore, please comply with our regulations. There are some rules that every learning center must follow. First, there must be time to respect the Thai national flag every morning. Students must sing the Thai national anthem as Thai students in Thai schools usually do. Another rule is that there must be portraits and photographs of the King and the Queen in every learning center. Every learning center must have at least two hours of Thai language class each week. These are what every center must do.

> Regarding Thai class, this is because everybody is to stay in Thailand for a long time. Therefore, communication in Thai should be encouraged in every learning center. If the children do not understand Thai, there will be communication problems between them and Thai people. Students also must learn about the lifestyle of Thai people and Thai laws. For example, Thai people drive on the left while Burmese people drive on the right. You are required to know our basic laws at least.

This statement demonstrates that the Thai authorities intend to turn migrant schools almost into "Thai" educational institutions where symbolic practices in association with Thai nationalism must take place. An emphasis also lies on national security, as indicated in his speech.

> Our office needs to take national security into account, listen to national security institutions' concerns and apply them for our well-being of ourselves......When you come to live in Thailand and run learning centers, we try our best to take care of you. The vital thing to be emphasized here is that learning centers must not instill any antagonistic sentiment or political philosophy against the government of our neighboring countries. We want to provide education for migrant children to enhance their knowledge and ability so that they can live in Thailand. However, it is not an opportunity for you to introduce political ideas. Rather, you should teach something like "What is democracy?", "How does democracy work in our country?" and so forth. If the teaching instigates conflicts, it is not supported.

His statement shows that while the state promotes migrant

education, it remains conscious of security and worries that migrant schools could be ideological havens for anti-Burmese government activists who have already concentrated in Mae Sot. Whether security issues come first or humanitarian ones come first is unsettling (Premjai 2011). Sometimes this issue causes friction and tension among the government ministries, particularly between the Ministry of Interior, for which regulation comes as imperative, and MOE, for which more or less educational interests come as important. The deputy director of the ESAO 2 told me that it was hard to compromise the conflicting interests.

The state is now sharing the assets of migrant schools, and its status has been changed from an informal non-state institution to a formal state institution. It might be interpreted that the state displayed power against migrant leaders and NGOs, exercised the state's sovereignty, and eventually brought migrant schools under its control. However, from an alternative stance, the engagement of the state reflects the impressive growth of the migrant education institution to the degree that the state has no option but to engage in the institution. In other words, the migrant institution has brought the state into play and has achieved recognition from the state as a legitimate formal institution.

Reactions of Migrant Education Leaders and NGOs

In the beginning, many migrant education leaders and NGOs were skeptical of the real intentions behind the government's involvement in migrant and refugee education. Some NGOs interpreted the government's move, through MOE, as an attempt to take over the stakes of education and place it under their total control, thus displacing the migrants and the NGOs from their current positions. For instance, in the monthly meetings of the CCSDPT in May and June of 2005, educational NGOs highlighted this as a significant issue. Some of them felt that the move towards equipping the Burmese refugees and migrants with the ability to speak the Thai language aimed at employing them as a source of cheap labor. Others pointed out that in the long term, the expanded influence of the Thai government in the lives of the Burmese could give the government greater leverage, even in issues like the repatriation of refugees and migrants. Furthermore, what seemed like an attempt to nurture the migrants and refugees as potential collaborators in education could be a government strategy to appropriate the educational methodologies of the migrant schools. Therefore, these NGOs wished to keep the government at bay in migrant education and informally run migrant schools.

Burmese migrant leaders were not sure of the government's new and different stances at the outset either. Fear factors did not disappear in their minds, even in the face of the seemingly benevolent attitude of the government. The government's positive attitude was considered contradictory given that the government continued to enforce legality in the town by using physical threats.

The government sometimes showed an inconsistent attitude in dealing with migrant schools, which questioned the government's sincerity. For example, in February and March of 2006, the Thai authorities closed five schools in Phop Phra District because the schools were operating without permission from local authorities and posed a potential threat like the religious schools in southern Thailand (Federation of Trade Unions Burma 2006; Irrawaddy 2006b).

Thai advocates staged a counter-action against this government action. For instance, on March 19, 2006, Thai Senator Jon Ungpakorn led a delegation to Mae Sot to meet several NGOs and assess the migrants' conditions. He then promised to draw up a proposal to improve the living conditions of the migrant workers. Speaking on the closure of the migrant schools, he mentioned that citing national security as the reason for closing the schools was unreasonable. He also stated that the educational opportunities for migrant workers and their children needed to be expanded (Irrawaddy 2006a; 2006b).

Nevertheless, the basic direction taken by the government for migrant schools was shared by migrants and NGOs through various meetings. Migrant school administrators who participated in a series of meetings with Thai officials considered the government's new approach an improvement and felt optimistic about the move. Paw Ray, the chairperson of BMWEC and headmaster of Hsa Thoo Lei School, mentioned in Irrawaddy (2006c), "In the past, we always worried about when they will come and close our school down, but this concern has become less now." Her statement shows that migrant people think of the registration of migrant schools as one of the ways to secure their security, given their illegal status so far. When the schools are registered, they are also offered an identity card by the Thai authority. Indeed, the Thai authority provided registration cards to the teachers of existing schools.

She also said in the report, "I have sat in five or six meetings with them [Thai officials] and I think things are improving." In the face of this development, administrators from the Burmese schools intended to register their schools as Learning Centers following the guidelines laid by the government. However, it is difficult for them to follow all the suggestions put forward by the Thai officials, such as hiring qualified Thai teachers, since it causes them a substantial cost. Indeed, in the gathering between the officials of ESAO 2 and migrant teachers on January 14, 2010, migrant participants raised this issue to the office's director but did not hear a clear vision. Despite controversial issues such as this, overall, migrants welcomed the state's move towards migrant schools. As mentioned before, it is mainly because this move could stabilize their stay more than ever.

Migrant education leaders were willing to cooperate with the state and share their assets. In this willingness, the migrant education institution became formal to a certain degree in the state system. They cannot now claim sole ownership of the institution, and the notion of independent migration education became an old story. Consequently, the identity problem of migrant schools would become a serious concern and would not be easily settled. Still, in the absence of accreditation for the graduation of migrant schools, the future of migrant students after graduation is uncertain. The barometer of the genuineness of the state would lie in accreditation for migrant education.

Conclusion: Institution and Integration

This chapter has dealt with migrant schools, highlighting development history, their connections or relationships with other partners, and the state's engagement in migrant education. It has shown that the dramatic growth of migrant schools has improved the condition of the migrants' settlement. With migrant schools, they came to live relatively secure lives despite the lack of proper legal status. The establishment and operation of migrant schools resulted from their connections with other partners from refugee camps, international NGOs, and Thai locals. These relationships were an intrinsic part of the formation and operation of migrant schools and engendered what can be called a "migrant institution."

The building of this migrant institution was possible without any need for state involvement in its operation. Despite being a non-state institution, it was visibly and massively rooted in the everyday lives of migrant people. The migrant schools' roles extended beyond education, acting as administrative and social units where migrants attached a sense of belonging though they were undocumented.

The growth of the migrant institution eventually brought the state into play as one of the stakeholders. This study has described the background of the state's involvement and recent policies. The key to these policies was registering migrant schools as regular learning centers, and relevant regulations have ensued. In the face of this move, migrant education leaders were initially cautious of the movement but later followed the regulations since they could give them a kind of legal status. Although the government might be the sole winner, migrants can secure a more stable residence while riding on this move.

The critical concept recurring throughout this paper was institution-building, which improves our understanding of migrants' coping strategies and the state's engagement. Migrant schools are focal areas where concerned agencies participate in institution-building. They opened up a space for each of the stakeholders to interact. At first, institution-building began in collaboration with migrants and NGOs. Later, the state participated in this institution-building, and a new chapter began in the history of the migrants' settlement.

This institution-building is novel and challenging, not just for the migrants themselves but also for the state. Conventionally, education was understood as a component of nationalism and state formation (Anderson 2006). In the case of Thailand, the adoption of western education was profoundly associated with the modernization of the state (Wyatt 1994). The contemporary Thai state also used education to integrate frontier and rural areas into the state system (Chayan 1984; 1991). However, now "migrant education" as an alien element gives a different source in the state formation of Thailand. It shows how substantially the presence of others became embedded in the current phase of state-building in Thailand.

Recent attempts to integrate migrant education into the Thai education system should not necessarily come as a victory of the state over the migrants and migrant schools. If this were the case, the state has every reason to dismantle this migrant institution simply because it is "illegal." Unlike it, the migrant institution continues its presence. By welcoming another participant, the state, and expanding its scope to the national level, the migrant institution has become more visible and stable, educating migrant children and securing their stay. However, it would be challenging in the future for migrant schools to balance state influence and serve as a key institution for migrants in general. Migrant education is at this critical juncture as it is transitioning from the informal to the formal, from the illegal to the legal, with the state's involvement.

Chapter 6

A Migrant Clinic: Legitimacy, Partnerships, and Cross-Border Healthcare Mobility

Introduction

In this chapter, I examine how an unauthorized Burmese migrant clinic, named the Mae Tao Clinic (MTC) or Dr. Cynthia Clinic, in Mae Sot serves as an essential healthcare provider not just for migrants in the town but also people from Myanmar. Since its establishment as a makeshift clinic by Dr. Cynthia Maung and a small group of students in 1989 who crossed the border to escape the then-military regime's brutal crackdown on democratic movements, the clinic has increased its capacity and become an influential healthcare institution and the symbol of human rights advocacy in the border region over the years. Now it has developed to treat about 100,000 cases a year, nearly half of which are from the Myanmar side (MTC Annual Report 2019/2020). It clearly shows that the clinic promotes migrants' health in general and induces transnational healthcare-seeking of the Burmese across the border. Although officially "illegal," as in the case of migrant schools, it has become socially legitimate in the border town, strengthening partnerships with local, national, and international health organizations. The chapter argues that the partnerships provide a strong foundation so that the clinic can overcome illegality and vulnerability and generate cross-border healthcare mobility.

This chapter first discusses how the clinic provides a new source of theoretical understanding of migrant healthcare. Then the chapter explores the development history of the MTC. It is followed by a discussion of how the clinic has become a legitimate health institution in the local society. Moreover, it investigates how it treats migrant patients in their everyday lives in Mae Sot, thus forming a community. It also deals with how it provides medical treatment across the border, engaging in cross-border patient mobility and medical services. Lastly, the paper considers transnational partnerships that have strengthened the clinic's capacity.

"Illegal" but Legitimate Healthcare Institution

The MTC provides a unique case in studies of migration in general, migrants' healthcare, and transnational healthcare-seeking because this unauthorized migrant clinic was initiated and has now run under the ownership of migrants themselves, providing healthcare services across the border. This study first builds upon structural approaches concerning how a host society's healthcare system integrates migrant patients (Castañeda 2012; Chavez 2012; Marrow 2012; Pavlish et al. 2010; Seo 2016; Viladrich 2012). Scholars critically review structural discrimination and racism (Huffman et al. 2012; Viruell-Fuentes et al. 2012) and medical policies of entitlement and exclusion (Mladovsky 2009; Sargent and Larchanché 2011). The vulnerability of unauthorized migrants, children, and women in this discriminatory system attracts particular attention (Adanu and Johnson 2009; Dettlaff and Rycraft 2010; Johnson and Marchi 2009; Willen 2012; Wolf et al. 2005). Scholars point out that even legal migrants, who are entitled to the healthcare system of host societies, cannot afford to pay for medical treatment, and many obstacles, such as language problems, clinicians' attitudes, and uncomfortable environments, restrict their access to the healthcare providers of host societies (Holmes 2012; Horton 2011).

In the unfavorable environments of host societies, migrants' health conditions deteriorate. Overall, the primary concern of this structural approach to migrants' health conditions tends to center around the domestic healthcare system of host countries that discriminate against migrants.

Like other migrants, Burmese migrants in Mae Sot also experience similar restrictions in the Thai healthcare system. In particular, they live unstable lives exposed to arrest and deportation and encounter many obstacles, such as language problems in their pursuit of medical treatment in the host society. However, what distinguishes them from others is that they do not necessarily rely on the Thai healthcare system but have an alternative health institution. Thus, even though the host society's healthcare system discriminates against them, they can quickly pursue medical treatment in the MTC. Indeed we can find similar cases in other countries, such as Israel (Gottlieb et al. 2012) and Germany (Castañeda 2009), where migrant clinics treat migrant patients. However, in Israel, establishing and operating an "open clinic" was solely initiated by domestic humanitarian NGOs, not migrants themselves. In Germany, too, German volunteers, not migrants, set up and run a "Berlin clinic" to treat unauthorized migrant patients. The building trajectory of the MTC sharply differs from the two cases where migrants' role in the establishment and operation of the clinic is not conspicuous. Migrants played a crucial role in creating and operating the MTC even in a precarious situation.

This point leads to another stream of research that emphasizes migrants' agency apart from the aforementioned structural approach. This agency-centered approach sheds light on how migrants maintain and seek healthcare despite structural constraints. Here scholars pay attention to the transnational healthcare-seeking strategies of migrants. Their behavior can be divided into two types. One type is that patients, while staying in a host country, maintain and consume the home country's traditional remedies, such as herbal medicines and spiritual consultation. This behavior is seen in the cases of southern African migrants in London (Thomas 2010), Surinamese migrants in the Netherlands (van Andel and Westers 2010), Karen migrants in Thailand (Bodeker and Newmann 2012), and Bengali immigrant women in New York (Chakrabarti 2010) through "transnational therapy networks" (Krause 2008).

The other type is that patients return to their home country or go elsewhere to seek healthcare treatment in a more affordable, comfortable, and perhaps effective environment, as seen in the cases of Mexican migrants in the United States (Bergmark et al. 2010; Brown 2008; Chavez et al. 1985; Wallace et al. 2009), Korean immigrants in New Zealand (Lee et al. 2010), and Cape Verdean immigrants in the Netherlands (De Freitas 2005).[60]

The MTC epitomizes the cross-border patient mobility or transnational healthcare-seeking that the agency-centered approach highlights. The clinic caters to the needs of migrants in Thailand and also to those of Burmese patients from the other side of the border. However, the context where cross-border patient mobility takes place in the clinic is very different from other cases. In other

---

60 This type can be related to the medical tourism sector, where people pursue cross-border health treatment. However, as Glinos et al. (2010: 1146) mention, "the industry-driven term 'medical tourism' insinuates leisurely traveling and does not capture the seriousness of most patient mobility" across the border. Thus they suggest the term "cross-border patient mobility" and define it as "the movement of a patient traveling to another country to seek planned healthcare."

cases, it is typical for people in the host societies to return to their home countries to seek health treatment in a familiar context. Mexican, Korean, and other ethnic immigrants in the cases above adopt this pattern. In contrast, in the case of the MTC, people in a home country cross the border to seek health treatment in the unauthorized migrant health institution of their nationals in a foreign country. It also differs from typical cases of medical tourism, where patients travel to another country to seek health treatment in a foreign healthcare institution. It is a case never dealt with in the existing studies of transnational healthcare or migration in general. The uniqueness of the MTC expands the scope of understanding migrants' health treatment and transnational healthcare-seeking.

How has the migrant clinic become a prominent medical institution for the Burmese on both sides, generating cross-border healthcare mobility? Given that illegality often associates with deportability and temporality (De Genova 2002), the MTC's persistent presence calls for an investigation of its constitution. Here, building upon Abraham and van Schendel (2005), I put forward an alternative distinction that concerns the "licit" or what is socially legitimate, and the "illicit" or what is otherwise beyond the legal-illegal categorization to understand the constitution of the migrant clinic. Although "illegal" according to legal standards, the clinic is "licit" and accepted as a legitimate institution in the particular locality. The clinic has strengthened its legitimate position by practicing humanitarianism that often invalidates the state's regulation in the context of the emerging discourse of "health as human rights" (Meier and Onzivu 2014).

The clinic's case features a crucial aspect of the global political economy that overcomes nationalistic binary divisions between the legal and illegal. Humanitarianism, particularly in healthcare, empowers a refugee doctor to legitimize her medical treatment, opens up an opportunity for the state to promote its humanitarian image by allowing the clinic's operation, and induces global players such as NGOs to engage in the less-privileged clinic. This entanglement that the global norm promotes has consequently developed into partnerships that legitimize the clinic's presence despite its illegal status. Alongside this global norm, I identify a geographical factor that concerns the Thailand-Myanmar border. Unlike statist approaches, I emphasize that the border mediates cross-border mobility and promotes transnational networks. While standing at the border, the clinic plays a prime role in generating cross-border healthcare mobility. This mobility, in turn, strengthens the legitimate presence of the clinic. I argue that this legitimacy encourages migrants to practice their agency in building up the clinic and seeking healthcare, although I do not dismiss structural conditions that influence the trajectory of institution building and the pattern of their healthcare-seeking.

Development of the Mae Tao Clinic

The establishment of the MTC[61] was directly related to political instability in the latter part of 1988 when the military took power and brutally cracked down on democratic movements. A Karen

61 This section mainly draws from a book that commemorates the 20th anniversary of the Mae Tao Clinic (2010) as well as Dr. Cynthia Maung's various speeches and interviews that I observed and conducted during my stay in Mae Sot.

medical doctor named Cynthia Maung fled with a group of her colleagues to Thailand to seek sanctuary. At first, they arrived in a nearby area of the current Mae La refugee camp, which is 60 kilometers north of Mae Sot. After working at a small hospital for a month or so, Cynthia's group moved to Huay Ka Loke refugee camp[62] 10 kilometers north of Mae Sot. While staying there, they collaborated with Karen leaders, local Thai authorities, and church groups to organize more treatment for refugee patients. Eventually, in February 1989, they opened a makeshift medical clinic on the dusty outskirts of Mae Sot.

At that time, the clinic had virtually no supplies, no money, and no medical staff (except Cynthia Maung) formally trained in medicine. Furthermore, they were staying in Thailand illegally and did not speak Thai. Thus, the clinic was expected to only run for a short while. At a meeting I attended on December 8-9, 2004, Cynthia Maung recalled, "When I started the clinic, I thought it would run for three to four months." She and her colleagues hoped the military junta would negotiate peace talks with pro-democracy groups and ethnic minorities under international pressure. However, that was not realized, and the clinic's history unfolded on the Thai side of the border.

From the beginning, the MTC stood in partnerships with various organizations. Among the first groups were Mae Sot Catholic Church and Christ Church Thailand, which arranged safe accommodation and helped the clinic establish initial partnerships with the Mae Sot Hospital. International partners such as Médecins Sans Frontières,

62 This camp was attacked by the Burmese military in 1997 and 1998 and subsequently moved to Umphiem Camp, a newly built camp 87 kilometers south of Mae Sot in 1999 (Human Rights Watch 2007).

Planet Care, Global Health and Access Program, Brackett Refugee Education Fund, and Burmese Relief Center extended crucial assistance to the clinic. Ethnic groups and pro-democracy groups cooperated with the clinic from the early days. Indeed, the clinic was the first outcome of cooperation between ethnic resistance groups and the All Burma Students' Democratic Front (ABSDF). Some students were founding members; others joined the clinic as medics and staff. Among Karen civil groups, the Karen Department of Health and Welfare was a crucial partner in delivering healthcare inside Myanmar. In addition, the Burma Medical Association, an interethnic cooperation group, cooperated with the clinic to provide medical care in ethnic areas and organize various training programs. Above all, the Mae Sot Hospital was an indispensable partner. Initially, the clinic could do little more than dress minor wounds and treat simple malaria; all severe cases were referred to the Mae Sot Hospital (MTC 2010: 35).

In the mid-1990s, the clinic became more stabilized and expanded its capacity and facility. Development included the issue of delivery certificates in 1994, setting up a maternal child health program in 1995, and a blood lab in 1996 to screen pregnant women for HIV, hepatitis B, and syphilis. In 1998, the child outpatient department officially opened. In 1999, as the patient population grew, inpatient departments became more specialized and divided into medical, pediatric, reproductive health, and trauma/surgery inpatient departments (MTC 2010: 39-56).

The MTC continued to build up its capacity in the early 2000s. The dental clinic was set up in 2001 as an adjunct to the clinic's surgery department. Now it has substantially developed an administrative sector as well. It began using an electronic database program for its inpatient department in 2000 and came to centralize the database transmitted from each of the clinic's departments by 2004. In 2003-04, the public health authority of Tak Province helped the clinic improve its database's ability to monitor major infectious diseases. With the advancement of the database system, the work of the department of registration and medical records improved. In addition, to efficiently expand and strengthen partnerships, it formed a public relations center in 2003 (MTC 2010: 61-79).

Throughout the latter part of the 2000s, the clinic broadened its scope. In 2006, the counseling center was officially opened in a new building, and mental health services became part of the primary healthcare in the clinic. In 2008, the infection prevention unit was set up, although its activities had started long before its official establishment. Until 2008, each clinic department had its own small pharmacy area. However, in 2008, a new central pharmacy was formed, and a networked computer system allowed each department to order medications from the central pharmacy (MTC 2010: 80-91). During the 2000s, the clinic strengthened partnerships with international and local organizations. I often heard Dr. Cynthia emphasize these partnerships as a cornerstone to strengthen its presence and promote health conditions when she delivered speeches on various occasions.

The impressive development of the clinic throughout the years is illustrated in Figure 3, which shows the increasing caseload.

<Figure 3> Yearly Caseloads of the Mae Tao Clinic

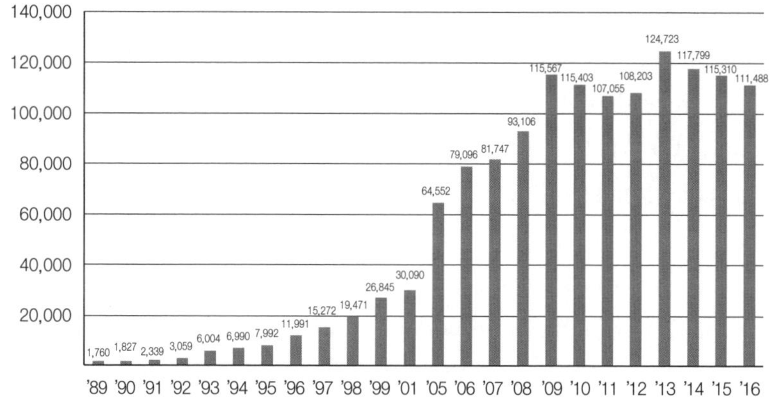

Sources: Mae Tao Clinic Annual Reports from 1989 to 2016

In the first year (1989), the clinic dealt with 1,760 cases. From then on, it constantly increased up to 2009, when it dealt with 115,567 cases. The number of cases then stabilized between 100,000 and 125,000 from 2010 to 2016. Nearly half of the patients were from Myanmar; for instance, in 2016, among 54,521 total clients, the number of clients from Myanmar was 25,950, comprising 48% (MTC Annual Report 2016: 18). It demonstrates the clinic has played a crucial role across the border.

Legitimate Presence in the Locality

Despite impressive growth, the clinic remained "illegal" because Dr. Cynthia Maung did not hold a medical license authorized by the Thai authority. The clinic was established without legal permission from the host state. Thus, the Thai authority could easily dismantle it. When I met the head officer (*nay amphoe*) of Mae Sot District on May 8, 2005, I asked how he viewed the clinic. He answered, "I know the clinic is illegal. I could arrest them. But I let them run the clinic since they do good things for society." From a humanitarian stance, the MTC is tolerated by the Thai authority. Indeed local Thais that I met showed great respect for Dr. Cynthia Maung. Bunni, one of my Thai informants, told me on February 4, 2014, "Cynthia is very famous. She is more famous than anyone in Mae Sot in the world. Her name is more widely known to the outside than Mae Sot." Somsak, Anan, and other local Thais, whom I have associated with, also showed great respect for her humanitarian work, although all of them knew about the unauthorized status of the clinic. In a conventional understanding, "illegality" is often associated with clandestine, unstable, and, in the end, deportable activities (De Genova 2002). However, the "illegal" MTC has been open and persistent since its establishment. Humanitarian activities have legitimized the clinic's presence in the eyes of local Thai people and even the authorities.

Above all, close cooperation between the MTC and the Mae Sot Hospital from the beginning has contributed to the clinic's legitimate presence and operation, which the clinic acknowledges,

> Considering that MTC is not a legally recognized establishment in Thailand, the level of support it has received from the Mae Sot Hospital (MSH) and the Ministry of Health (MoH) is remarkable. The local support provides a certain amount of stability, and thus the ability of work effectively (MTC 2010: 36).

The director of the MSH also acknowledges the achievements of the clinic, saying,

> Mae Tao Clinic has successfully been providing health services to the migrant population, which normally has poor access to healthcare. We have been working and supporting each other to reduce the health burden in the population since the establishment of the clinic. The cooperation between the clinic and the Mae Sot General Hospital has long been excellent (MTC 2010: 35).

Since 1989, a medical referral program between the two sides has been operating. For instance, in 2016 too, a total of 862 referrals, about 0.8% of cases to MSH (MTC Annual Report 2016: 22). However, the clinic was not a free rider in the Thai health institution. For instance, referrals cost the clinic 14.2 million baht in 2012, representing 25% of the clinic's health expenditure in 2012 (MTC Annual Report 2012: 32). The Thai Public Health Ministry said that most of the hospitals in the five provinces along the border shouldered the burden of providing healthcare services to migrant workers and non-Thais crossing the border (Nation 2013). Indeed, the MTC shoulders the burden to a great extent. The Thai health authority would have to bear a more significant burden in its absence. The Thai authority sometimes relies on the clinic to implement policies, including a recent drug rehabilitation project. The probation department under the Ministry of Justice consulted with Dr. Cynthia on the project. Probationers can seek counseling as well as medical treatment from the clinic (Bangkok Post 2014a).

Alongside the practical cooperation between the clinic and the Thai authority, the visits of people in high offices to this "illegal" clinic strengthen its legitimate position as a humanitarian institution. For instance, former Thai Prime Minister Abhisit Vejjajiva visited and encouraged the clinic on December 6, 2012. At that time, the clinic took the opportunity to explain the health situation at the border and its activities (Karen News 2012).[63] The clinic used this visit to emphasize its presence in the border town as an indispensable health institution to the border society, accommodating migrants and cross-border health-seeking travelers.

On the other hand, the host society uses the clinic's recognition to promote its image as a guardian of humanitarianism, as we can grasp from the statement of the head officer of Mae Sot District and the visits of people in high offices. Indeed, not just for those officials and politicians but also for local Thais, the clinic has become a popular destination to observe how humanitarianism works in their locality and how they are benign enough to let this unauthorized clinic operate. It has become a humanitarian site for field trips. I often encountered groups of Thais, including students, who visited it for that purpose. Though unauthorized, the presence of this humanitarian health institution provides a source of promoting self-esteem for Thais in general.

The clinic has done good things for local Thais at a practical level, including creating many job opportunities. The entrance to the clinic is full of Thai motorbike taxi drivers and food vendors who rely on migrant and cross-border patients for their livelihood. Thai motorbike taxi drivers and bus drivers at river piers are always busy transporting Burmese patients to the clinic. Ironically, the livelihood

63 See also Burma Children Medical Fund (2012: 31-33). http://burmachildren.com/wp-content/uploads/2013/04/Burma-Children-Medical-Fund-Annual-Report-2012.pdf, accessed June 7, 2015.

of many local Thais is heavily dependent on this "illegal" clinic.

To sum up, alongside the main factor of the clinic's partnerships with local and international health institutions, humanitarian appeal and practical contributions have provided a strong foundation as a legitimate institution in the local society.

Migrants and the Clinic

Indeed, legal migrants are entitled to the Thai health insurance scheme. As of 2016, the health insurance fee was 2,200 baht per year. In addition, migrants need to pay 600 baht as the health examination fee. Thus it costs an adult migrant 2,800 baht to access the insurance scheme (Yan 2016). Apart from this, the Thai government has initiated a new scheme--the social security board card--which costs 8% of a worker's wage, half of which employers pay. Migrants entitled to this scheme pay 550 baht for health insurance and 600 baht for health examinations, in total 1,150 baht (IOM 2013).

However, in any scheme, the fee is not affordable for migrants given their income levels, ranging from 3,000 to 6,000 baht per month. In the case of the social security board card scheme, employers are reluctant to contribute 4% for each person. In addition, unfriendly hospital environments, language barriers, and consequent communication difficulties with Thai doctors all discouraged seeking health treatment in Thai hospitals. Thus, the structural constraints prevented migrants from accessing Thai health institutions.

I often associated with Seni and Tamul, who were Karen migrants, had work permits, and were thus entitled to the Thai health insurance scheme. However, each time they were sick, they went only to the MTC and never considered Thai clinics or hospitals as an option. First, they were not confident speaking Thai before Thai doctors. Their choice was also partly influenced by their fear of the Thai authorities, particularly the police that intimidate, arrest, and deport unauthorized migrants. Migrants, unauthorized or legal, have been exposed to this intimidation in their everyday lives. Since the late 1980s, when migration took place on a large scale, the police have often checked migrants and deported "illegal" ones. Fear is deeply ingrained into their mind regardless of legality. Although legal migrants have access to Thai hospitals, they cannot be comfortable in them. Thus, Seni and Tamul, though legal migrants, deliberately choose the MTC where they feel at home, can easily communicate, and are only charged the registration fee of 30 baht[64] without additional payment for any treatment. They are even provided with food and shelter for free during their stay in the clinic.

Unlike Seni and Tamul, Hserku and Gido held no legal documents. The married couple lived in a makeshift house in a migrant compound and earned some money by taking care of the buildings of a Karen church. One day Hserku became pregnant and made regular visits to the MTC for prenatal checkups. Eventually, she gave birth to a daughter at the clinic on January 29, 2005. A few days later, many people from a Karen community with whom the couple and I often associated came to the clinic to see her and the

64 The registration fee was introduced in 2006 to have patients keep their registration chart under the same name; otherwise, they easily change their names, partly because of security reasons (Interview with a MTC staff, February 6, 2014).

newborn baby. They chatted with each other, and the baby was the source of their happiness. It was evident that the social bond among Karen migrants strengthened, centering on the clinic. Indeed, the clinic has served as an important community center for migrants in general, accommodating the visits of family members, relatives, friends, and villagers. It has also organized cultural events such as a New Year's festival and promotes a sense of community for migrants beyond simply providing medical treatment.

Those migrants hired as domestic workers and thus do not closely associate with migrant communities also rely on the clinic for their health treatment. In this case, their Thai employers encourage and send them to the clinic. In February 2014, I revisited my former Thai landlord, who had been hiring the same Burmese worker for over ten years. I was very familiar with the worker as I had often talked to him during my initial stay in the mid-2000s. The landlord told me, "My employee was sick a couple of days ago and got treatment in the MTC. He always goes there whenever he is sick." The Thai landlord appreciated the clinic for always taking care of his employee.

A study of Burmese female factory workers shows that most gave birth in the clinic (Pearson and Kusakabe 2012: 162). All over Mae Sot, whether migrants are living within a community or individually making a living, whether they are unauthorized or not, it is usual for them to go to the clinic. This story does not just apply to migrants. Those Thai Karen who do not have a Thai identity card also seek healthcare treatment at the clinic. Refugees who temporarily stay in the town outside of refugee camps rely on the clinic.

The clinic contributes to the constitution of migrant lives in the locality regardless of legality. Apart from treating migrant patients, the clinic regularly reaches out to migrant schools located in migrant compounds and conducts various types of programs, including first aid treatment and basic hygiene and sanitation education to promote the health condition of the migrants and their living environments. For instance, on April 1, 2014, the staff of the clinic offered first aid training to 45 students in the migrant Thoo Mae Kee school, raising awareness about communicable diseases (tuberculosis, pneumonia, diarrhea, worm infestation, malaria, and dengue fever), and HIV/AIDS. All of this evidence indicates that, in general, the clinic has become an indispensable health institution for migrants in Mae Sot. Furthermore, it highlights that the presence of the clinic has stabilized the presence of migrants whose life otherwise might have been fragile in the lack or absence of proper treatment.

Cross-Border Healthcare Mobility

As mentioned earlier, about half of the patients are from the Myanmar side of the border. In 2016, 25,950 out of 54,521 clients were from Myanmar (MTC Annual Report 2016: 17). The reason behind this cross-border healthcare-seeking is apparent. "[The] health sector in Myanmar still fails to provide most basic health services for patients. Although the national health budget has increased fourfold for 2012/2013, most of the new budget was for salaries. Health attracts less than 3% of overall government expenditure" (The Lancet 2012: 2313). Life expectancy remains at 56 years and 40% of all Myanmar children under the age of 5 years are moderately stunted. The country has more than half of all malaria-related deaths in Southeast Asia.

Furthermore, most health services are concentrated in larger cities, although most live in rural areas. Rural patients often travel to big cities like Yangon, but this is unaffordable. Widespread corruption and a lack of reliable health indicators prevent the development of the healthcare system (Bangkok Post 2013). The option for people, particularly in rural areas along the border, is to cross the border to seek healthcare in the MTC. The clinic is well-known all over Myanmar. Even doctors in Yangon recommend that some patients go to the clinic, said a clinic staff member.

The story of a seven-year-old boy, Saw Paw Yaw,[65] whom I met in February 2014, exemplifies the trajectory of cross-border healthcare-seeking. He was born with the help of a traditional birth attendant at home in No Nae village, Karen State, in Myanmar. When he was a few months old, he often became sick with fever, coughing, and fatigue, so his parents took him to the medic in their village. The medic did not diagnose his condition well, and thus Saw Paw Yaw received medication for his apparent symptoms. However, this did not work, and his condition became more severe. He was then sent to a traditional healer for a massage with holy water, but this did not help either. In October 2012, his grandmother took him to Pa-an Hospital, and he underwent various checkups. The results showed that he had a heart problem. The doctor at the hospital said that Saw Paw Yaw needed heart surgery but must wait until he grew up and could get surgical treatment in Yangon. In the meantime, his parents

65 I saw him on February 5, 2014, and heard the story from the Burma Children Medical Fund, which has an MTC office and closely cooperated with it.

left for Bangkok to find better jobs, and his grandparents had to take care of him. His symptoms did not improve, and hospital costs became unaffordable. When he was next very sick and blue, his grandmother decided to bring him to the MTC. She asked for help to come to Mae Sot as she had to pay for transportation services. When he eventually arrived at the MTC on July 10, 2013, the clinic realized this was a severe case and referred the child to a large hospital in Chiang Mai, where, after an operation, he recovered.

As in the case of Saw Paw Yaw, people inside Myanmar first seek treatment in local clinics and then move to a hospital in a big city. However, the lack of hospital facilities, delayed treatment, and unaffordable hospital fees put a significant burden on them. Eventually, they often cross the border to seek treatment in the MTC. The case highlights that the MTC's presence encourages people under domestic structural constraints to practice their mobility across the border.

On the one hand, people in Myawaddy and its vicinity have relatively easy access to the clinic because there are no critical geographical restrictions on their journey to the clinic. With proper travel documents, they can cross the bridge and get on a bus that frequently operates between the border post and the clinic. Some patients, particularly pregnant women about to give birth, arrange a private car directly from Myawaddy to the clinic. People without legal documents cross the river by boat and get a bus from the pier to the clinic. It is an everyday scene that the front gate of the clinic is crowded with buses, motorbike taxis, and passengers. It seems part of everyday practice for people in Myawaddy and its vicinity to cross the border to receive medical treatment at the clinic. Their cognitive and healthcare-seeking scale extends beyond the state boundary. The clinic activates and accelerates this transnational patient mobility.

Meanwhile, the MTC regularly sends mobile medical teams inside eastern Myanmar, including to Karen, Mon, and Kayah states, and particularly to areas that international humanitarian organizations cannot reach to provide primary healthcare. The clinic began sending the teams in 1996 in response to serious humanitarian crises there caused by increased attacks from the Myanmar government. It cooperated with many groups of ethnic health workers and eventually became a cornerstone in forming the Back Pack Health Worker Team in 1998.[66] After training in the clinic, the mobile medics carry and distribute medicine to internally displaced people inside Myanmar, sometimes conducting basic operations on the spot. They also provide food and school textbooks (Horstmann 2011: 514). In addition to dispatching these medics, the MTC has set up a remote clinic, the Pa Hite clinic, in Karen State, where the MTC provides medicines and supplies. Sometimes, the Pa Hite clinic refers severely ill patients to the MTC.

The MTC has strengthened cross-border healthcare cooperation among ethnic groups and offered medical training to ethnic medics. After completing the programs, they return to their areas and continue cooperating with the MTC. This interethnic cooperation resulted in the formation of the Health Convergence Core Group in May 2012. The members include Chin, Karen, Kayah, Mon, and Shan ethnic health organizations, BPHWT, the MTC, the National Health and Education Committee, and the Burma Medical

---

66 See the webpage of the BPHWT (http://backpackteam.org/?page_id=31, accessed June 22, 2015).

Association. Through this cooperation, cross-border healthcare mobility has strengthened (Health Information System Working Group 2015: 12). These activities show that the MTC has been pivotal in promoting cross-border mobility among patients and ethnic groups inside Myanmar.

Transnational Partnerships

One day in February 2014, I saw that the eye treatment department was far more crowded with patients than usual. I asked a staff why it was so. He answered, "It is time for an eye surgeon from Scotland to operate, and thus more patients come here. The Scottish surgeon visits the clinic around this time every year." Next to the eye department, I saw a Taiwanese acupuncturist treating patients. A Korean acupuncturist whom I know of worked there in 2015. In 2016, 27 foreign volunteer doctors were working in the clinic (MTC Annual Report 2016: 39). While staying there, they concentrated on conducting operations and, at times, training sessions. Medical students from many countries undergo internship programs. In 2016, the clinic hosted medical students from 18 universities in various countries, including Australia, the UK, the USA, France, and Sweden (MTC Annual Report 2016: 51).

Above all, international partners provide considerable financial support to the clinic. These groups include the International Rescue Committee, USAID, Norwegian Church Aid, Burma Relief Centre, AusAid, Terre Des Hommes-Netherlands, the Open Society Institute,

Global Fund for Malaria, and Union Aid Abroad-APHEDA.[67] In addition, individual donors regularly or irregularly support the clinic. This financial support from foreign organizations and individuals has empowered the clinic to expand its capacity even under precarious conditions.

Besides medical and financial support, many foreigners work as technicians, researchers, administrators, and advisors. For instance, foreign volunteers work on annual and other reports published in English. Others work on public relations, running social network services such as Facebook and the Internet homepage. Apart from volunteers, other foreign visitors, including students, journalists, human rights activists, and others, stop by the clinic to observe activities.

What draws particular attention is that foreign Christian missionaries and churches actively assist the clinic. It is partly associated with the fact that the religious background of Dr. Cynthia and many staff, particularly Karen staff, is Christian. Indeed, we can see the widespread influence of Christian missionaries and churches along the border who, from the clinic's early days, have engaged in helping displaced people (Horstmann 2011). Above all, missionaries and churches from Asian countries, including Korea, Taiwan, Singapore, and the Philippines, have strengthened relations with the clinic. Korean missionaries and churches are outstanding among them. For instance, a church in Seoul dispatched a missionary whose main work centers on the clinic. He has mediated collaborations between the clinic and Korean churches, delivering assistance and,

67 According to the clinic's financial report in 2013, the amount of funding from foreign partners is 106.6 million baht, a dominant revenue source for the clinic.

at times, guiding the summer field trips of church groups to the clinic. His activities are regularly updated and announced among his church members back in Korea.

However, there have been some contentious issues over collaborations with foreign partners. For one thing, different management styles between native staff and foreign volunteers sometimes create tension and dispute. As the clinic relies on foreign assistance, its administration and governance are influenced and constrained by them. Furthermore, it is difficult to coordinate and regularize the engagement of foreigners who come from various groups and countries. Another issue is that the foreign connection has promoted the exodus of individual medics in the clinic to a certain degree. I witnessed this in particular in the mid-2000s, when large-scale resettlement programs began, and many medics departed the clinic. Some individuals may have taken opportunities to restart their lives in foreign countries with the support of foreigners. Obviously, from the clinic's perspective, this represents a drain of human resources, although the clinic soon recovered with another group of medics and staff moving from Myanmar. From a different perspective, this shows that transnational flows of resources, including even the exodus to third countries, are part of the constituents of the clinic.

Transnational partnerships have intensified as Dr. Cynthia has visited various countries. For instance, Dr. Cynthia visited the USA in March 2015 and delivered at the UCLA Fielding School of Public Health. She visited Korea to receive Ilga Foundation Award and deliver speeches, including one at Yonsei University at my invitation in September 2015. Dr. Cynthia again visited Korea to receive

Gwangju Prize for Human Rights in May 2022. She has indeed become a symbol of human rights in Asia and beyond. On every occasion, she has emphasized the MTC's legitimate presence on the border and its collaborations with partners. Her overseas visits also aim to promote fundraising. Her fame has contributed to the clinic's sustenance in expanding and consolidating transnational partnerships.

However, during Myanmar's democratization, international organizations turned their attention and funding from the clinic and refugees to inside Myanmar in the expectation that migrants and refugees would return to their home country. For instance, Australia's confirmation that AusAid would not continue funding shocked the clinic (Karen News 2013). The clinic tried to diversify funding sources and persuade international organizations to keep paying attention to the plight of migrants and refugees. It overcame the clinic's funding crisis due to the combined efforts of the concerned parties. Paradoxically the Coronavirus pandemic and Myanmar's military coup in the early 2020s have restrengthened the clinic's role in combatting the epidemic and recent refugee influx, calling for a more concerted transnational partnership.

In the lack or absence of legality and resources, the MTC has used transnational partnerships to cope with the state and build up its capacity. The MTC knows how to ride on the wave of global human rights movements that are useful in legitimizing and strengthening its position.

Conclusion

I have demonstrated how the MTC has evolved as a conspicuous healthcare institution in Mae Sot and its vicinity over the years. Although it started as a humble clinic in 1989 after its founders escaped political turmoil in Myanmar, it has built up its capacity to deal with over 100,000 cases a year. What mainly draws our attention is that although it is technically illegal, it has become licit, socially legitimate in local society (Abraham and van Schendel 2005). The recognition of the clinic as a legitimate institution first developed from partnerships with local healthcare authorities and the appeal of human rights to Thai officials and politicians. In practice, the clinic benefits many local Thais and creates job opportunities, which strengthens its licit position in local society. Meanwhile, the clinic has developed partnerships with various transnational organizations and individuals, which have become essential resources in its finance and operation.

The case of the MTC expands the understanding of migrants' healthcare-seeking in general. Unlike conventional studies that often emphasize the structural constraints of the host society's healthcare system that discourage migrants' use, this study highlights the agency migrants have developed in their own healthcare institution even in the face of structural restrictions. The MTC story also sheds new light on understanding transnational patient mobility. While conventional cases concern the return of migrant patients to their origin (e.g., Lee et al. 2010), the MTC case demonstrates the migration of patients in their country of origin to an unauthorized migrant clinic in the host country. The different directions and patterns also inspire us to rethink the association between class and transnational medical mobility (Connell 2006; 2013; Sobo 2009). Cross-border healthcare mobility is not just the story of affluent patients but also that of less privileged ones. The legitimate presence of the migrant clinic in the border town mediates and strengthens less privileged people's healthcare mobility across the border. Above all, partnerships with various individuals and organizations that promote health as a human right have empowered the clinic to undertake a legitimate role in the border society despite the absence and lack of proper legality.

Indeed, the democratization of Myanmar put the clinic at a critical juncture. Refugees along the border were expected to return home (Reuters 2014). International donors focused more on the development inside Myanmar than on assistance to refugees and migrants. The funding crisis that the MTC once experienced reflected the changing political situation in Myanmar. The Coronavirus pandemic and the coup in Myanmar in the early 2020s posed a new challenge for the MTC. How would the clinic carry on its mission in the face of such crises? The clinic continues to be at the border town rather than returning to Myanmar. It finds its rationale as a healthcare institution at the border where it can continue to mobilize and strengthen collaborations with various ethnic, national, and international partners. As in its history, partnerships will play essential roles in its future. In particular, in the process of regional integration in the name of the ASEAN Community, the clinic is expected to take care of the likely explosion in the number of migrants (Bangkok Post 2014c). The clinic will continue to be at the central stage of transnational healthcare mobility of underprivileged migrants in collaborative partnerships.

Chapter 7

Mobility Practices: The Bangkok Dream, Resettlement, and Borderland Dynamics

Introduction

The arrival, temporary stay, and departure cycles of Burmese migrants and refugees have dramatically impacted Mae Sot. For many migrants, Mae Sot is not a final destination but a transit point. They attempt to migrate to Bangkok for better opportunities. At the same time, refugees staying in nearby camps moved to third countries, including the USA and European countries.

Here I revisit theoretical discussions of the Introduction, particularly on moving people and border mediation. I seek to offer an alternative to the approaches that consider places as discrete, separate, and self-reliant and that view people's lives as being formed and maintained in these particular places. Appadurai (1996) and others (e.g., Gupta and Ferguson 1997) have criticized that these conventional approaches tend to incarcerate natives to a particular place spatially and ignore relationships with and influences from the outside. Particularly in the era of globalization, there is a need to consider the mobile features of people's modes of life. Therefore, "migrants" and "refugees" became proper subjects to epitomize the very nature of mobility in the post-modern era. Borderlands also drew attention as an "adequate conceptualization of the 'normal' locale of the post-modern subject" rather than "as insignificant, as marginal zones, thin slivers of land between stable places" (Gupta and Ferguson 1997: 48).

However, seemingly post-modern subjects cannot avoid the influence of the modern nation-state. The state tends to appropriate the borderland to mark the symbol of its sovereignty firmly. Nevertheless, the roles played by the periphery in power relations between the center and the periphery cannot be ignored completely. State-centric approaches presuppose that peripheries would eventually be incorporated into political, economic, and cultural centers. Although these state/center-centric approaches are informative in understanding the nature of the center's power and influence on the peripheries, they oversimplify power relations.

In contrast to the state-centric framework, I reaffirm that borderlands play an active role as a "node" in interconnecting national boundaries. I agree with Hannerz (1996: 17), who identifies that "the interconnectedness typically takes the shape of a relatively continuous spectrum of interacting meanings and meaningful forms, along which the various contributing historical sources of the culture are differentially visible and active." In this interconnectedness, borderlands have become the places where "interplay" and "mixtures," or "creolization," between the center and periphery take place. In borderlands, absolute distinctions between "we" and the distant "they" are blurred and "transnational" mobility is prominent (Kearney 1991: 55). This theoretical discussion applies to Mae Sot. Mae Sot plays an interconnecting role across and beyond the border as a border town and entry point between Thailand and Myanmar. Burmese migrants exploit this connectivity by moving from Myanmar to Mae Sot, Bangkok, and other countries.

The concepts of node and interconnectedness epitomize key features of border social systems: fluidity, vibrancy, and movements. The constant ebb and flow of people is a regular phenomenon in borderlands and an intrinsic part of the border society. Alvarez (1984: 121) states that a social system or society is built upon organized, fluid movements of people through time and space. He (1984:

121) mentions that these fluid people are the lifeblood of societies and that migration and mobility are organized parts of these social systems. According to him (1984: 122), "the flow of people through a continuing migration (legal, undocumented, temporary, permanent, circular, and so on) is built into the fabric of border society." Fluidity does not necessarily destabilize the social system in the borderlands. Instead, it is an inherent part of the formation of the border society. Then and now, Mae Sot has played and continues to play a role as a transit point for different types of migrants, transients, and people on the move. When some people leave to pursue better opportunities elsewhere, another group will soon fill the void. It demonstrates that fluidity and migration are deeply associated with the border society.

In the following sections, I first discuss the "Bangkok dream," which I coined to characterize the pattern of onward movement by migrants from Mae Sot to Bangkok in pursuit of economic goals. It is followed by a discussion of resettlement programs that pave the way for refugees to migrate from the border area to other countries. In discussing the Bangkok dream and the migration to third countries, I show how these forces generate population movement across and beyond the border.

The Bangkok Dream

Nukphan, with whom I maintained regular contact, took over ownership of the factory from a Thai owner in 2000 and ran a garment factory with 420 workers, mostly Burmese, on her payroll. She filled production orders from Bangkok, subcontracting from global brands such as Nautica. Over the years, she encountered the continual loss of her employees to Bangkok. She revealed that in 2004, around 110 workers, which comprised over twenty-five percent of her entire workforce, left her factory, mostly heading for Bangkok. The trend continued throughout the 2010s, although the number varied depending on Bangkok's economic situation and job availability.

Another Thai factory owner, Suanpha, who ran a garment factory in Mae Sot, producing clothes for the Reebok brand, also disclosed that around ten percent of her 120 workers had departed her factory in the middle of the 2000s. Most of them also headed to Bangkok. Farms and shops experienced the same problem. Paradon, who was running a rose farm, mentioned that several workers had quit his farm to move on to Bangkok in 2005. He saw the Burmese using Mae Sot as a learning ground, after which they moved on to other places,

> Mae Sot is like a kindergarten for the Burmese, where they learn how to adapt to Thai society. It is the place where they learn the Thai language and culture before leaving for larger places.

I did observe the fast turnaround of workers in restaurants and shops, which I regularly visited. Many workers I knew were no longer around whenever I revisited Mae Sot. This situation could be partly due to the agreement between the Governor of Tak and other provinces to transfer Burmese workers from Tak Province to provinces with labor shortages. For instance, a fishing net factory in Khon Kaen Province was granted a quota to hire 1,800 foreign workers after the factory manager requested to hire foreign workers from Tak Province. The factory's request was approved, and the transfer occurred on November 15, 2004 (Bangkok Post 2004e). Some policemen and officials were believed to have exploited the implementation of this policy to their advantage. They often extorted brokerage bribes from the Burmese migrants, and even gangs were involved in this movement of workers (Bangkok Post 2005c). This policy motivated ordinary Burmese workers, whether or not they were holding valid work permits, to seek better opportunities in other places beyond the border.

The factory owners in Mae Sot stood against this policy. On August 29, 2005, they held a demonstration at the District Office of Mae Sot seeking to revoke the policy. Following the demonstration, the policy was abandoned. However, according to an official in the Mae Sot Labor Office, nevertheless, the unauthorized movement of Burmese laborers to Bangkok and other places around Thailand continued, initiated by migration networks between the Burmese migrants and brokers and also between the border town and Bangkok. Information on available jobs, housing, and temporary support in Bangkok spread among the Burmese workers in the border town through the networks.

What draws the Burmese migrants in Mae Sot to Bangkok? Many migrants mentioned more job opportunities and relatively higher wages that encouraged their movement to Bangkok. According to Nukphan and Suanpha, in 2010, an individual Burmese laborer hired in their factories earned around 130 baht a day compared with around 200 baht a day in Bangkok. This wage gap is a compelling reason to move on from Mae Sot for ordinary Burmese laborers. It is understandable why jobless Burmese and temporary workers in small-scale construction sites would be keen to get a job in Bangkok to solve their precarious living conditions.

Cultural reasons also explain Burmese migration from Mae Sot to Bangkok. The more attractive metropolitan environment certainly attracts them to Bangkok, which I heard from migrants. Their friends and relatives in Bangkok convey stories describing the global city's advanced lifestyles. These narratives spread in the factories of Nukphan and Suanpha and the teashops, motivating the Burmese to go after the Bangkok dream.

Mae La camp, near Mae Sot, is also a staging point for migration to Bangkok. According to refugees in the camp, each family typically had at least one family member working in Bangkok. They estimated that some ten percent of all camp residents were working in Bangkok, with a similar number working in nearby areas, including Mae Sot. Limited job opportunities in the camp compel refugees to move elsewhere. The regulations of the Thai government do not allow refugees to work outside the refugee camps. Nonetheless, many refugees sneak out to Mae Sot to work. A UHNCR official in the Mae Sot Field Office revealed to me on April 12, 2005, that one of the main activities of the office is to bring the refugees who are arrested by the Thai police back to the refugee camps.

The Burmese migrants moving to Bangkok often encounter various obstacles in their journey. For instance, they must pass through several checkpoints guarded by soldiers and police officers on the road between Mae Sot and Tak. According to interviews with Burmese migrants, some migrants attempt to climb the rugged mountain rather than travel by car to evade these checkpoints. Once they get to Tak, it is relatively easy for them to take a car and head for Bangkok since there is no checkpoint between Tak and Bangkok. Some of them even walked from Mae Sot to Bangkok. Walking the distance of 509 km takes several days. Refugees from Mae La camp allegedly climbed a nearby mountain and walked along mountain pathways to an inland town and then onto the main road, where they boarded a car arranged to take them to Bangkok. Some refugees indicated that this route is more secure and convenient than the direct Mae Sot-Tak passage.

While some Burmese I interviewed used these methods to avoid the checkpoints on their way to Bangkok, many relied on brokers. In 2010, brokers' fees for a guaranteed safe passage to Bangkok could amount to more than 10,000 baht per person. Those who lacked sufficient funds could borrow money from the brokers and pay off their debt through monthly salary deductions. As mentioned earlier, some officials and gangsters were involved in this affair. Recruiters often deceive some migrants with others to move them to Bangkok. One of my informants said that recruiters told him they would bring him to Bangkok. However, he ended up in Pattani, a province in southern Thailand. He had to work in the fishing industry for months, with his entire monthly wage going to his recruiters to repay his debt. Eventually, he was arrested by the police and sent back to Mae Sot to be deported to Myanmar.[68]

When Burmese migrate to Bangkok, the migrants' families suffer from displacement. Family members become separated.

---

68 For general information on human trafficking in Thailand, see the International Labour Organization (ILO) (2005).

When parents go to Bangkok to work, the children remaining in Mae Sot may lack proper care. Although some migrant schools run dormitories for such children, sufficient care is lacking due to inadequate staff and funding. In addition, elderly Burmese do not receive care from their children working in Bangkok, even though remittances help solve financial difficulties to some degree. In the case of factories, farms, and shops, the loss of workers to Bangkok discourages owners from operating businesses legally. Workers' departure means losing expenses the owners advanced for their employees' Work Permit applications. As a result, employers are very reluctant to have their new employees apply for Work Permits for fear that they will leave soon before they can recover the expenses of obtaining the Work Permits. It partly explains the low compliance rate to policies governing foreign workers' economic activities in Mae Sot.

Despite this outflow of people from Mae Sot, Mae Sot's social system, including the economic sector, has not collapsed because a continuing inflow of people from Myanmar counterbalances the steady outflow of migrants. For the Burmese inside Myanmar, Mae Sot is like an extended territory of Myanmar that they can reach with relative ease. Similar to the networks between Mae Sot and Bangkok, networks exist between Mae Sot and the adjacent Burmese areas. These networks often develop among kin groups and townmates. Through these networks, news of job opportunities in Mae Sot continues to spread in Myanmar, and the Burmese continue to come to the border town. However, they do not pursue a permanent settlement in the border town; instead, they set their sights on Bangkok for better opportunities. The circulation of population movement does not necessarily destabilize the town. Instead, the coming and going of people have become an intrinsic part of the border society.

Resettlement Programs

Resettlement programs also generate population movement from the borderland. These programs have significantly impacted urban refugees called "Persons of Concern (POCs)"[69] in Mae Sot and camp-based refugees. Since Burmese migrants tend to stay together and live in the same migrant neighborhoods as political refugees, they can be familiar with resettlement programs.

When the UNHCR, in cooperation with some Western countries such as the USA, Canada, Norway, Sweden, and Australia, first implemented these resettlement programs in early 2004, only those POCs staying outside the refugee camps were eligible to apply for resettlement in a third country. By the middle of 2005, the resettlement programs governed by the UNHCR came to include other (i.e., non-POC) refugees in the camps. Before this expansion, there were individual cases of refugees resettling in other countries under the sponsorship of individuals and organizations in resettlement countries and the concerned governments' approval. However, since 2005 these foreign governments have opened their

69 Since the Thai government is not a signatory to the 1951 UN Convention and 1967 Protocol on Refugees, asylum seekers in Thailand are technically regarded as "illegal immigrants" under the national law. However, the Thai government often refers to Burmese refugees as "displaced persons" (*phu opphayop*) (Lang 2002: 92-93). In particular, those who fled into Thailand for political reasons and stay in the urban areas are referred to as "Persons of Concern."

doors to many Burmese refugees. In 2005, the Thai government approved for third countries to offer resettlement programs to registered refugees in all camps along the border (TBBC 2008: 4).

103,257 Burmese refugees became resettled in third countries from 2006 to June 2015, as Table 6 shows. The USA is ranked the most, followed by Australia, Canada, and Finland, while Japan began the program in 2010. South Korea also did it by bringing Burmese refugees in December 2015.[70]

<Table 6> The Number of Resettled Burmese Refugees, 2006-2015

Country / Year	USA	Australia	Canada	Finland	Norway	New Zealand	Sweden	Nether-lands	UK	Ireland	Japan	Denmark	Others	Total
2006	2,681	757	794	208	355	201	357	115	81	0	0	7	5	5,561
2007	10,436	1,520	1,611	383	460	158	212	96	111	97	0	9	9	15,102
2008	14,406	1,563	697	308	84	25	143	189	29	0	0	1	7	17,452
2009	13,033	2,332	874	240	297	116	134	27	5	0	0	11	10	17,079
2010	10,013	1,011	350	129	51	5	89	100	4	3	27	16	31	11,829
2011	8,137	794	82	179	13	171	21	108	0	2	18	4	14	9,543
2012	6,553	377	28	158	16	153	16	95	0	0	0	0	18	7,414
2013	7,553	919	81	137	27	104	1	75	1	0	18	9	89	9,014
2014	5,809	953	187	1	3	47	22	163	3	1	23	3	61	7,276
2015*	2,358	453	71	0	1	97	1	6	0	0	0	0	0	2,987
Total	80,979	10,679	4,775	1,743	1,307	1,077	996	974	234	103	86	60	244	103,257

*January-June

Source: TBC 2015: 10

The departure of refugees under the resettlement programs enticed economic migrants to also avail of opportunities to migrate to foreign countries. Indeed, the UNHCR Mae Sot Field Office has

70 I witnessed the arrival of 24 Burmese refugees at Incheon Airport in South Korea on December 23, 2015.

had to handle frequent visits from ordinary people asking about the programs. I observed that Burmese migrants regularly approached the office to inquire about the application processes. An individual who passes the procedure through documents screening and an interview by the UNHCR becomes a POC. The individual then has to apply for the resettlement program and undergo other processes, including interviews conducted by the embassies of the concerned countries in cooperation with the UNHCR. Those who succeed in passing the embassy interviews are also required to pass a medical checkup and attend cultural orientation sessions where they learn about the lifestyles of their intended destinations. Upon completing all these requirements, they then depart for Bangkok, and from there, they transfer to their destination countries.

In the resettlement programs, the status of the POC is essential since the POCs are eligible to apply for resettlement programs and receive special support from the host countries. For the Thai government, these resettlement programs that enable the removal of persons who pose security threats to Thailand are welcome solutions to the country's security problem. Indeed, the Thai government moved the POCs out of urban areas to refugee camps by March 31, 2005, notably to the Noh Poe camp in Umphang District, where they had to stay until they left for third countries. It took this action to prevent Burmese political activists from engaging in political activities in the urban areas of Thailand (Bangkok Post 2005a; Irrawaddy 2005b). Urban refugees were transferred to the camps in 2006 (Irrawaddy 2006e).

Through the resettlement programs, many Burmese, especially political activists, have departed for other countries 600 Burmese exiles with UN documents left the so-called "Liberated Area" in 2004, according to a report (Irrawaddy 2005a). In the case of the National League for Democracy (NLD), as many as 100 members left the border for third countries between 2003 and June 2005, with 250 members remaining in Mae Sot and its vicinity border areas as of June 2005. Additionally, many of the remaining members of the NLD applied for resettlement programs. As membership in the NLD was regarded as a guarantee for selection, Burmese migrants who had not been associated with it began to apply for membership to gain an advantage in the selection process for the resettlement program. In the case of the Mae Sot-based Assistance Association for Political Prisoners, 21 of the 100 members of the organization resettled in 2004 in the USA and Norway, while the rest have applied for UN refugee status and are likely to follow (Irrawaddy 2005a). The All Burma Students' Democratic Front also saw about sixty members opting for resettlement from 2005 to 2006, although it maintained the rule of forbidding members to apply for UN refugee status to maintain the group's strength (Irrawaddy 2006d). As of 2010, almost all the original members had departed from the border.

The reasons for applying for the resettlement programs reflect political activists' adversities in their everyday lives. They had to endure extremely harsh living conditions in the Thailand-Myanmar borderland in the hope of restoring democracy in Myanmar. However, the country's political situation never improved, and they lost hope that political change would occur. Furthermore, their lack of financial stability and unstable living conditions increased the hardships they experienced, prompting their application for resettlement. The prospect of escaping hardships and beginning a new life in developed countries made it extremely difficult for many to resist such an opportunity.

Other reasons for the resettlement programs surfaced. Many young applicants mentioned a lack of educational opportunities as a decisive factor in their application for resettlement. They had not acquired a proper education in Myanmar or Thailand. They expected that resettlement would allow them to pursue higher education under the sponsorships of the concerned governments. For many of the parents, the educational prospects for their children motivated them to apply for the resettlement programs. I often heard from the parents that they could stay in the borderland but wanted their children to have better educational opportunities in third countries.

However, the elderly refugees were not as interested in the resettlement programs as the young since they were afraid of adapting to a totally new environment and language. Nonetheless, many older generations dutifully followed their sons and daughters to other countries rather than face aging alone in the borderland. Some of the elderly, especially those with high levels of education, even applied for the resettlement programs themselves to live a more comfortable life and receive a government pension.

Economic opportunity was another reason for resettlement. A refugee complained that they were not paid for their work at the construction site of a refugee camp, saying, "If I go to a foreign country, even toilet cleaning work will bring me seven dollars per hour." This statement demonstrated the knowledge held by the refugees about the outside world and their attempts to seek further opportunities to improve their livelihood beyond the refugee camps. Many applicants for resettlement expected future economic prosperity in the resettlement countries. Their departure, however, did not mean severing their ties to the borderland; some interviewees said they would continue to support their organizations in the border financially.

The resettlement programs impact individuals, organizations, and communities. Individuals may regard resettlement as a blessing that opens up numerous opportunities, despite the imminent challenges faced in adapting to the host societies. However, organizations and communities considered the programs a disaster due to the resulting brain drain. As discussed above, political movements and groups lost many members through the resettlement programs. The educational system in the refugee camps was also adversely affected because of the departure of qualified teachers. I felt NGOs' frustration at the meetings held in June and July 2005 by the Coordinating Committee for Services to Displaced Persons in Thailand, a representative of NGOs helping the Burmese refugees. Many NGOs revealed that their refugee employees had left their organizations and commented that finding suitable teachers to fill their positions was difficult. Many Karen organizations, such as the Karen church, Karen Women's Organization (KWO), and Karen Youth Organization, also experienced a loss of members. The General Secretary of the KWO sarcastically lamented when I spoke with her on January 14, 2005, "Now we are returning to the Stone Age in the absence of educated people. What we will learn in the future is just how to make fire using stones."

Indeed, it is evident that the resettlement programs are reducing the capacity of the KNU. An NGO worker remarked, "For the KNU, the real threat does not come from the Burmese government but from the UNHCR and Western countries." It became difficult for the KNU to find committed young people. Soldiers were deserting the battlefields in the face of immediate opportunities for a better life. Even the soldiers of the Democratic Karen Buddhist Army (DKBA), which broke away from the Christian-dominated Karen in 1994, knew about the resettlement programs and tried to avail themselves of resettlement opportunities. For instance, during my visit to the Umphang District border area in Thailand, a DKBA soldier in charge of Burmese areas near Umphang District shared with one of my Karen informants that he was interested in the resettlement programs himself.

One of the high officials in the KNU expressed his concern about the negative impact of the resettlement programs, stating, "It is a real danger for the KNU given that educated people depart from the organization." On the other hand, he countered this by saying, "Not all people are leaving, and those resettled would make some contributions in the future."

People working with refugees, particularly NGOs and Karen community leaders, are divided in their opinion about the resettlement programs. The overriding question for those who support resettlement is how to carry on the nation's missions or achieve political change with the loss of human resources. The overriding question for those opposing resettlement is what alternatives individuals have under prolonged hardships, which can lead to tension between the competing notions of individualism and communalism. The massive interest in resettlement programs suggests that individualism is winning over communalism. Political leaders are torn between their political convictions, on the one hand,

and wanting to provide a better life for their children, on the other.

Refugee resettlement programs have generated enormous population movement, driving out refugees from Mae Sot to third countries and pulling Burmese migration to Mae Sot. Many people crossed the border and came to Mae Sot from inside Myanmar, such as Yangon, to approach the UNHCR and the refugee camps to take advantage of resettlement opportunities. Once they applied for refugee status with the UNHCR in Mae Sot, they continued to stay in the town, engaged in livelihood activities, or participated in group activities while waiting for interview appointments and screening results. Even if their cases were rejected, many did not want to return to Myanmar.[71] One of the reasons I often heard was that the Burmese authorities would interrogate them regarding their application with the UNHCR.

The resettlement programs attracted Burmese people to the refugee camps near Mae Sot. The UNHCR began a registration program in October 2004 in cooperation with the Thai government's Ministry of Interior (MOI). The program started in camps in the southern part and extended northward to the camps in Tak Province in 2005. Coincidently, the resettlement programs were expanded to the refugee camps during this period. Upon hearing about the registration, many Burmese attempted to get into the camps to register to qualify for resettlement. However, the main objective of the registration program was to re-register the original camp population to arrive at an exact count. In registering new people, although the UNHCR and the MOI were responsible for registering

71 Here we see the categories of economic migrant and refugee are somewhat fluid, especially in a particular place like Mae Sot, where political refugees and economic migrants coexist.

the names, the Provincial Admissions Board decided on the entitlement of camp residents. In other words, the asylum seeker status of those who registered and their subsequent resettlement chances were not confirmed. Whether they knew about the processes or not, it did not stop them from attempting to get into the camps by whatever means. Interestingly, some Thai Karen living in villages near the refugee camps were also interested in the resettlement programs. They tried to get into the camps through ethnic connections with Burmese Karen refugees.

The registration program also enticed many refugees pursuing their livelihoods elsewhere to return to the camps. Thai police detained some returnees at the checkpoint close to the entrance of Mae Sot.

Above all, resettlement programs accelerated the population movement from Myanmar to the refugee camps. Although more than 100,000 refugees had already left the border by the end of June 2015, the total number of residents in the refugee camps never decreased but remained at a similar number, around 110,000 (TBC 2015: 6-10). People, whether "genuine" refugees or not, kept coming to the camps from Myanmar (or elsewhere in Thailand) to seek resettlement opportunities.

The population movement created by refugee resettlement programs reflects the current migration phase. The present movement pattern differs from that in the past when migration occurred without the involvement of international agencies. The social system of the border town has become much more fluid, vibrant and dynamic due to the resettlement programs introduced by the UNHCR and Western governments. They played an essential role in generating population movement across and beyond the border.

Conclusion

This chapter has examined how the Bangkok dream and resettlement programs accelerated migration from Myanmar to Mae Sot and, subsequently, to Bangkok and beyond. In their pursuit of a better livelihood, the desired destination of the Burmese migrants is not limited to Mae Sot but extends beyond the borderland, notably to Bangkok. The border town is a temporary nurturing place for them to adapt to Thai society, after which they move on to other places. Mae Sot serves as a receiving or host community and an embarking point without necessarily undermining the social system of the borderland. Mae Sot's role as a node in pursuing the Bangkok dream is illustrated in Figure 4.

<Figure 4> Migration Flows Generated by the Bangkok Dream

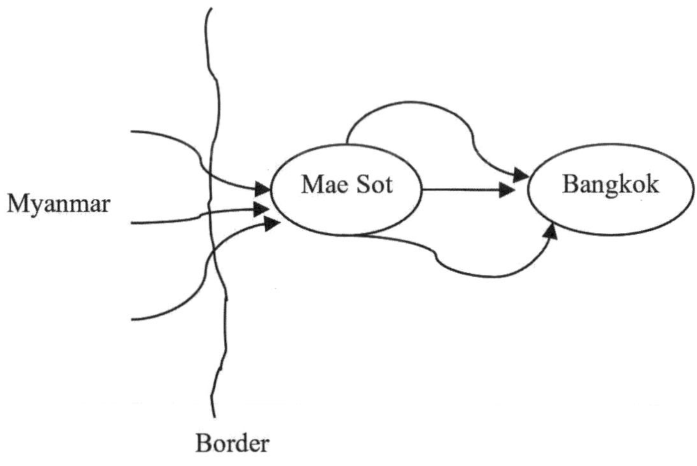

The participation of global actors such as the UNHCR and Western governments in addressing refugee problems added a new dimension by providing opportunities for resettlement beyond the Thailand-Myanmar borderland. The migration generated by resettlement programs reveals the impact of human rights on the borderland, where political activists and refugees are prominent. Figure 5 illustrates the migration generated by resettlement programs.

<Figure 5> Migration Flows Generated by Resettlement Programs

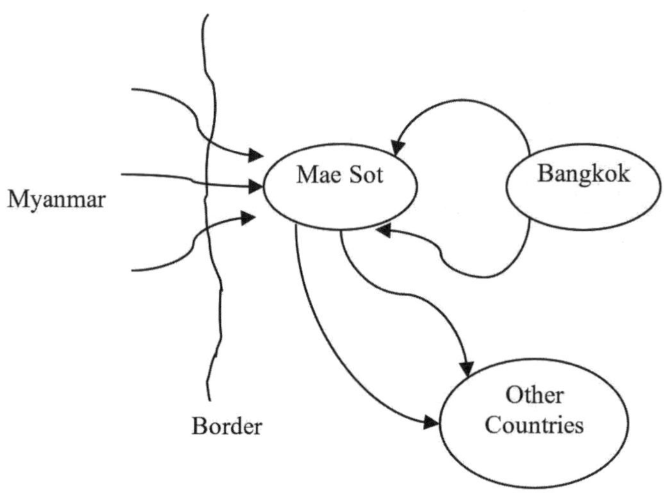

As in the case of the Bangkok dream, resettlement programs induce people inside Myanmar to migrate across the border. However, these programs also induce migrants and refugees to return to Mae Sot from Bangkok to pursue resettlement opportunities. The constant ebb and flow of people shape the societal formation of the border town. Attracted to other promising opportunities, migrants embark on further movement while a new set of migrants arrives and contributes to the maintenance of the social system of the borderland.

Chapter 8

Conclusion

I have explored how others prevail in the social system of the particular border town and its vicinity. The town cannot sustain itself without the participation and contribution of others. I have attempted to overcome the conventional description of others as victims and, thus, passive actors. In the common understanding, the roles of others in operating the social system are either absent or rarely recognized. This understanding mainly comes from the assumption that the absence of legal status does not allow them to have a proper position in society and drives them to be vulnerable to physical threats from state authorities. Obsession with the existence of legality as a prerequisite for analyzing a particular society obscures the possibility that the social system can be possible in the absence or lack thereof. Unlike pathological approaches to illegal people's ways of life, this book attempted to make a deeper understanding of their lives and give credence and due recognition to them in forming the social system of the town in the borderland.

The case of Mae Sot explicitly vindicates the possibility that society does not solely stand on the legal base. Despite others being illegal, unofficial, or unauthorized, the town's society never becomes disarrayed. This book proposes that it is reasonably necessary to consider illegality as a norm in constituting the society to achieve an adequate explanation for the formation of the society in the town. Furthermore, it suggests that integrating these legal and illegal domains gives a holistic understanding of society.

The prevalence of illegality is very much due to the geographical traits of the Thailand-Burma borderland that do not seriously restrict people's cross-border movement. The two states have been limited in controlling the movement. Although state boundaries were delineated, we still witness that state domains have been flexible, demonstrating the legacy of traditional states (Rajah 1990: 127). Standing on this nature, Mae Sot, as a central place in the borderland, accommodated a unique social system that the flowing of alien people across the border played a significant role in establishing. In the border social system, distinguishing between the legal and the illegal is extremely difficult and meaningless since these two domains are pervasively integrated into the system. We have seen that any attempts by the state to implement the legal domain did not occur without discrepancy. In the border town, including the unofficial domain in almost every sector of the system is inherent.

The book traced the social system's development in the borderland to set a tone. In doing this, it disclosed that the town's history is the history of others. In the historical processes of the town's development from a mere passing point to a substantial settlement area, the migration of other ethnic groups played a significant role. They began to fill the place by establishing and developing the town throughout its history. Even the current stage of development relies on the contribution of others in every sector of the town.

Turning to Burmese migrant enclaves, I again challenged a conventional understanding preoccupied with migrants' miserable conditions, which prevents us from viewing them as human agents to overcome hardship and rebuild their lives, even in precarious situations. Migrants' lives are dynamic, intersecting illegal and legal domains, crossing international borders, and appropriating transnational connections. Migrant schools in enclaves act as educational institutions and administrative units. This governance provides a solid foundation for migrants to build their lives and pursue further opportunities elsewhere. Mobility and connectivity are catalysts in forming migrant enclaves as transnational conjunctural spaces. In the migrants' constant pursuit of better lives, enclaves facilitate their passage from Myanmar through Mae Sot to Bangkok and other countries. Transcending bifocal attentions between their home and adopted countries predominating in conventional transnational studies, these migrants imagine, practice, and actualize a multi-focal dimension in their transnational lives.

Then I highlighted behind-the-scenes informal economic activities focused on unauthorized riverbank Burmese merchants, the cross-border movement of goods, and the nexus of ethnic politics and border trade. Although unauthorized trade is labeled as smuggling by the state, it is *withi chiwit*, a way of life for Burmese merchants on the riverbank, and even recognized by local state agencies. The merchants rationally and deliberately decided to smuggle as part of their livelihood, and smuggled goods have legitimately catered to the needs of local people, demonstrating that smuggling is deeply integrated into the economy of the border. The cross-border movement of goods by boat also reveals that informal ways carry on border trade. It further suggests that the border is not entirely regulated by state agencies but by other social groups, notably ethnic groups.

I elaborated more on migrant schools. The substantial existence of migrant schools enables migrant children to have their education even without proper legal status. The growth of migrant schools was an impressive outcome of collaborations between migrants, refugee camps, Thai locals, and international partners. It meant building a migrant institution and advancing how migrants constitute their lives in a solid foundation. Since the mid-2000s, the Thai government has engaged in migrant schools to regularize them as learning centers under its guidance. I argued that it should not necessarily come as a victory of the state over the migrants and migrant schools. Instead, it shows the impressive growth of the migrant education institution, bringing the state into play and having achieved recognition from the state as a legitimate formal institution.

The Mae Tao Clinic also epitomizes the prominence of a migrant institution. Established in 1989, the clinic has developed its capacity and serves as an essential healthcare institution across the border. Despite its illegality, Thai authorities recognize its importance and collaborate with the clinic. As in the case of migrant schools, collaborations with various partners play significant roles in running the clinic. Unlike existing literature on the health of migrants, which concerns structural constraints, I emphasized migrants' agency in creating their healthcare institution through collaborative partnerships and highlighted the cross-border healthcare mobility of underprivileged patients. The legitimate presence of the migrant clinic in the border town mediates and strengthens their transnational mobility across the border. Partnerships with various individuals and organizations have empowered the clinic to undertake a unique role in the border society.

Finally, I explored how the force of mobility affected the border society. In particular, I examined two forces generating human flows: the Bangkok dream and refugee resettlement programs. The former pushes Burmese migrants from the border to Bangkok to pursue better opportunities, while the latter takes Burmese refugees from the border to other countries. These two forces create massive human flows across and beyond the border. I revealed that the border town is a node in this population movement. My emphasis is that human flows do not necessarily dismantle the border society but are inherent in the societal formation of the border town.

Throughout the chapters, the lives of others in various sectors of the social system have been illustrated. The central theme overarching these chapters is the integration of the informal and the formal in the border social system. Throughout this book, we see this integration in various sectors of the border society, such as the economy, education, and healthcare. Also, the book has demonstrated the dynamics of the border social system accelerated by population flow.

Indeed, my findings overcome the *homo sacer* or bare life thesis that has increasingly influenced scholarships on migrant/refugee lives over the years, spearheaded by Agamben (1998). The bare life thesis is preoccupied with legality as an essential constituent that makes humans human. In other words, those lacking legality stop being humans and become miserable. From this point of view, we rely entirely on the whims of the state defining human conditions. Notably, the state exercises absolute, sovereign power in the borderland, an exceptional space for illegal migrants and refugees who will be arrested or deported without legal protection. However, this book has delivered a different story of how "bare lives" attempted to overcome their precariousness, taking advantage of opportunities that the borderland mediates and provides. The borderland transforms them into legitimate human beings, and they transform the borderland into a vibrant social system. Mobility is a new weapon of migrants in navigating the multi-focal transnational world.

Bibliography

Abraham, Itty, and Willem van Schendel. 2005. "Introduction: The Making of Illicitness." In *Illicit Flows and Criminal Things*, edited by Willem van Schendel and Itty Abraham, 1-37. Bloomington and Indianapolis: Indiana University Press.

Adanu, Richard, and Timothy Johnson. 2009. "Migration and Women's Health." *International Journal of Gynecology & Obstetrics* 106(2): 179-181.

Agamben, Giorgio. 1998. *Homo Sacer: Sovereign Power and Bare Life*. Stanford, CA: Stanford University Press.

Aguilar, Filomeno. 2012. "Differentiating Sedimented from Modular Transnationalism: The View from East Asia." *Asian and Pacific Migration Journal* 21(2): 149-172.

Alvarez, Robert R. 1984. "The Border as Social System: The California Case." *New Scholar* 9: 119-134.

Anderson, Benedict. 2006. *Imagined Communities: Reflections on the Origin and Spread of Nationalism*. London and New York: Verso.

Anurak Phanthurat. 1998. *Mae Sot Nueng Roi Pi* [A Hundred Years of Mae Sot's History]. Mae Sot: Mae Sot District Office.

Appadurai, Arjun. 1996. *Modernity at Large: Cultural Dimensions of Globalization*. Minneapolis, MN: University of Minnesota Press.

Arnold, Dennis. 2004. "The Situation of Burmese Migrant Workers in Mae Sot, Thailand." Working Paper Series No. 71, Southeast Asia Research Centre, City University of Hong Kong.

———. 2006. "Capital Expansion and Migrant Workers: Flexible Labor in the Thai-Burma Border Economy." MA Thesis, Mahidol University.

Arnold, Dennis, and Kevin Hewison. 2005. "Exploitation in Global Supply Chains: Burmese Migrant Workers in Mae Sot, Thailand." *Journal of Contemporary Asia* 35(3): 319-340.

Aronowitz, Stanley, and Henry Giroux. 1993. *Education Still under Siege*. Westport, CT: Bergin and Garvey.

Asian Development Bank (ADB). 2001. *Preinvestment Study for the Greater Mekong Subregion East-West Economic Corridor Volume 1 Integrative Report*. Manila: ADB.

———. 2004. *The GMS-Beyond Borders: Regional Cooperation Strategy and Program 2004-2008*. Manila: ADB.

———. 2012a. *The Greater Mekong Subregion at 20: Progress and Prospects*. Manila: ADB.

———. 2012b. *The Greater Mekong Subregion Economic Cooperation Program Strategic Framework 2012-2022*. Manila: ADB.

Asian Migrant Centre. 2005. *Resource Book: Migration in the Greater Mekong Subregion*. Hong Kong: Asian Migrant Centre.

Aung Kin. 1983. "Burma in 1982: On the Road to Recovery." In *Southeast Asian Affairs 1983*, edited by Pushpa Thambipillai, 87-101. Singapore: Institute of Southeast Asian Studies.

Aung-Thwin, Michael. 2002. "Lower Burma and Bago in the History of Burma." In *The Maritime Frontier of Burma: Exploring Political, Cultural and Commercial Interaction in the Indian Ocean World, 1200-1800*, edited by Jos Gommans and Jacques Leider, 25-57. Amsterdam: Koninklijke Nederlandse Akademie van Wetenschappen.

Bailey, Kenneth D. 1994. *Sociology and the New Systems Theory: Toward a Theoretical Synthesis*. Albany, NY: State University of New York Press.

Baird, Ian G. 2010. "Making Spaces: The Ethnic Brao People and the International Border between Laos and Cambodia." *Geoforum* 41(2): 271-281.

Balčaitė, Indrė. 2019. "Networks of Resilience: Legal Precarity and Transborder Citizenship among the Karen from Myanmar in Thailand." *TRaNS: Trans-Regional and-National Studies of Southeast Asia* 7(1): 63-89.

Ball, Jessica, and Angela Dim. 2016. "Migrant Learning Centers on the Thai-Myanmar Borderland: Giving New Meaning to 'Live and Learn'." *Childhood Education* 92(3): 200-209.

Bangkok Post. 2002. "Address by Princess Maha Chakri Sirindhorn: Formal Post-Primary Education and Vocational Training." October 4.

———. 2004a. "Khin Nyunt Ousted, Put under Arrest." October 20.

———. 2004b. "Maung Aye May Put Heat on Wa." October 24.

———. 2004c. "Junta Crushes Mafia Unit: Khin Nyunt's Cohorts Targeted by Hardliners." October 27.

———. 2004d. "The Downfall of Gen Khin Nyunt." October 31.

———. 2004e. "Gangs Benefit from Labour Transfer Plan." November 18.

———. 2005a. "834 Burmese Report for Relocation." April 1.

———. 2005b. "Call to Demolish Islet, Settle Border Dispute." April 11.

———. 2005c. "Aliens Being Kept Out of the System." September 13.

———. 2006. "Former KNU Leader Gen Bo Mya Dies, 79." December 25.

———. 2009. "Literacy Has No Nationality: The Education of Stateless Children along the Thai-Burmese Border Remains a Problem in Search of a Solution." September 15.

———. 2010. "Border Battle Spurs Exodus: Thousands Flee to Thai Side as Clashes Erupt." November 9.

———. 2011. "Myawaddy Border Crossing Re-Opened." December 5.

———. 2013. "Myanmar's Healthcare System in Critical Condition." June 24.

———. 2014a. "Getting Clean in Mae Sot." January 25.

———. 2014b "Mae Sot SEZ (Special Economic Zone) to Give Fillip to Myanmar Border Trade." October 15.

———. 2014c. "Cynthia Muang Warns of Border Migrant 'Explosion'." November 14.

Bastian, Adolf. 2004 [1866]. *A Journey in Burma (1861-1862).* Bangkok: White Lotus.

———. 2005 [1867]. *A Journey in Burma (1863).* Bangkok: White Lotus.

Battersby, Paul. 1998/1999. "Border Politics and the Broader Politics of Thailand's International Relations in the 1990s: From Communism to Capitalism." *Pacific Affairs* 71(4): 473-488.

Baud, Michiel, and Willem van Schendel. 1997. "Toward a Comparative History of Borderlands." *Journal of World History* 8(2): 211-242.

Bergmark, Regan, Donald Barr, and Ronald Garcia. 2010. "Mexican Immigrants in the US Living Far from the Border May Return to Mexico for Health Services." *Journal of Immigration and Minority Health* 12(4): 610-614.

Bodeker, Gerard, and Cora Neumann. 2012. "Revitalization and Development of Karen Traditional Medicine for Sustainable Refugee Health Services at the Thai-Burma Border." *Journal of Immigrant & Refugee Studies* 10(1): 6-30.

Brown, Henry S. 2008. "Do Mexican Immigrants Substitute Healthcare in Mexico for Health Insurance in the United States? The Role of Distance." *Social Science & Medicine* 67(12): 2036-2042.

Burma Children Medical Fund. 2012. *Annual Report.* Mae Sot: Burma Children Medical Fund.

Burma Labour Solidarity Organization (BLSO). 2002. "The Struggle of Burmese Migrant Workers."

———. 2006. "Min-gala-ba: The Newsletter for Supporters of the Burma Labour Solidarity Organisation and Its School."

Bo Mya. n.d. "Yeo Tha Le Kho Phlo Eo Me Eo Tho Leo Yeo Eh Dho Pa Phla Oh"

[The True Experiences that I Like to Mention].

Bourdieu, Pirre, and Jean-Claude Passeron. 1990. *Reproduction in Education, Society and Culture*. London: Sage.

Bowles, Edith. 1998. "From Village to Camp: Refugee Camp Life in Transition on the Thailand-Burma Border." *Forced Migration Review* 2: 11-14.

Burmese Migrant Workers' Education Committee (BMWEC). 2009. "Annual Report, 2008/09."

Campbell, Stephen. 2018. *Border Capitalism, Disrupted: Precarity and Struggle in a Southeast Asian Industrial Zone*. Ithaca, NY: Cornell University Press.

Carreón, Gustapo P., Corey Drake, and Angela C. Barton. 2005. "The Importance of Presence: Immigrant Parents' School Engagement Experiences." *American Educational Research Journal* 42(3): 465-498.

Castañeda, Heide. 2009. "Illegality as Risk Factor: A Survey of Unauthorized Migrant Patients in a Berlin Clinic." *Social Science & Medicine* 68(8): 1552-1560.

———. 2012. "'Over-Foreignization' or 'Unused Potential'? A Critical Review of Migrant Health in Germany and Responses toward Unauthorized Migration." *Social Science & Medicine* 74(6): 830-838.

Castells, Manuel, and Alejandro Portes. 1989. "World Underneath: The Origins, Dynamics, and Effects of the Informal Economy." In *The Informal Economy: Studies in Advanced and Less Developed Countries*, edited by Alejandro Portes, Manuel Castells and Lauren A. Benton, 11-37. Baltimore, MD: Johns Hopkins University Press.

Chakrabarti, Ranjana. 2010. "Therapeutic Networks of Pregnancy Care: Bengali Immigrant Women in New York City." *Social Science & Medicine* 71(2): 362-369.

Chang, Wen-Chin. 2003. "Three Yunnanese Jade Traders from Tengchong." *Kolor: Journal on Moving Communities* 3(1): 15-34.

———. 2004. "*Guanxi* and Regulation in Networks: The Yunnanese Jade Trade between Burma and Thailand, 1962-88." *Journal of Southeast Asian Studies* 35(3): 479-501.

———. 2009. "Venturing into 'Barbarous' Regions: Transborder Trade among Migrant Yunnanese between Thailand and Burma, 1960s-1980s." *Journal of Asian Studies* 68(2): 543-572.

Chavez, Leo R. 2012. "Undocumented Immigrants and Their Use of Medical Services in Orange County, California." *Social Science & Medicine* 74(6): 887-893.

Chavez, Leo R., Wayne A. Cornelius, and Oliver W. Jones. 1985. "Mexican Immigrants and the Utilization of U.S. Health Services: The Case of San

Diego." *Social Science & Medicine* 21(1): 93-102.

Chayan Vaddhanaphuti. 1984. "Cultural and Ideological Reproduction in Rural Northern Thai Society." PhD Thesis, Stanford University.

———. 1991. "Social and Ideological Reproduction in Rural Northern Thai Schools." In *Reshaping Local Worlds: Rural Education and Cultural Change in Southeast Asia*, edited by Charles F. Keyes, 153-173. New Haven, CT: Yale University Southeast Asia Studies.

Cheng, Lu-Lin, and Gary Gereffi. 1994. "The Informal Economy in East Asian Development." *International Journal of Urban and Regional Research* 18(2): 194-219.

Chiang, Adeline Hsu Leen. 2002. "Beyond Humanitarianism: Power and NGO-Karen Refugee Relations." Honours Thesis, National University of Singapore.

Coedès, George. 1968. *The Indianized States of Southeast Asia.* Honolulu, HI: University of Hawai'i Press.

Colquhoun, Archibald R., and Holt S. Hallett. 1885. *Amongst the Shans*. London: Field & Tuer.

Committee for Promotion and Protection of Child Rights (Burma). 2009. "Feeling Small in Another Person's Country: The Situation of Burmese Migrant Children in Mae Sot, Thailand."

Conchas, Gilberto Q. 2001. "Structuring Failure and Success: Understanding the Variability in Latino School Engagement." *Harvard Educational Review* 71(3): 475-504.

Condominas, George. 1990. *From Lawa to Mon, from Saa' to Thai: Historical and Anthropological Aspects of Southeast Asian Social Spaces*. Canberra: Department of Anthropology, Research School of Pacific Studies, Australian National University.

Connell, John. 2006. "Medical Tourism: Sea, Sun, Sand and … Surgery." *Tourism Management* 27(6): 1093-1100.

———. 2013. "Contemporary Medical Tourism: Conceptualisation, Culture and Commodification." *Tourism Management* 34: 1-13.

Damrong Rajanubhab. 2001. *Our Wars with the Burmese: Thai-Burmese Conflict 1539-1767*. Bangkok: White Lotus.

Dauvergne, Peter. 1998. "Weak States, Strong States: A State-in-Society Perspective." In *Weak and Strong States in Asia-Pacific Societies*, edited by Peter Dauvergne, 1-10. Canberra: Allen & Unwin.

De Freitas, Cláudia. 2005. "'Health Has No Borders': Cape Verdean Immigrants in the Netherlands and the Transnational Quest for Healthcare across Europe." *International Journal of Migration, Health and Social Care* 1(1): 19-36.

De Genova, Nicholas. 2002. "Migrant 'Illegality' and Deportability in Everyday

Life." *Annual Review of Anthropology* 31: 419-447.

———. 2005 *Working the Boundaries: Race, Space, and "Illegality" in Mexican Chicago.* Durham, NC: Duke University Press.

———. 2013. "Spectacles of Migrant 'Illegality': The Scene of Exclusion, the Obscene of Inclusion." *Ethnic and Racial Studies* 36(7): 1180-1198.

Democratic Voice of Burma. 2012. "Myanmar: Tension Eases in DKBA Arms Dispute." February 28.

Derks, Annuska. 2013. "Human Rights and (Im)Mobility: Migrants and the State in Thailand." *Sojourn: Journal of Social Issues in Southeast Asia* 28(2): 216-240.

Dettlaff, Alan J., and Joan R. Rycraft. 2010. "Adapting Systems of Care for Child Welfare Practice with Immigrant Latino Children and Families." *Evaluation and Program Planning* 33(3): 303-310.

Donnan, Hastings, and Thomas M. Wilson. 1999. *Borders: Frontiers of Identity, Nation and State.* Oxford and New York: Berg.

Dudley, Sandra. 2011. "Feeling at Home: Producing and Consuming Things in Karenni Refugee Camps on the Thai-Burma Border." *Population, Space and Place* 17: 742-755.

Duncan, Christopher R., ed. 2008. *Civilizing the Margins: Southeast Asian Government Policies for the Development of Minorities.* Singapore: NUS Press.

Eldering, Lotty, and Jo Kloprogge, eds. 1989. *Different Cultures, Same School: Ethnic Minority Children in Europe.* Amsterdam: Swets & Zeitlinger.

Erickson, Frederick. 1984. "School Literacy, Reasoning, and Civility: An Anthropologist's Perspective." *Review of Educational Research* 54(4): 525-546.

Evans, Grant, Christopher Hutton, and Kuah Khun Eng, eds. 2000. *Where China Meets Southeast Asia: Social and Cultural Change in the Border Regions.* Singapore: Institute of Southeast Asian Studies.

Faist, Thomas. 1999. "Developing Transnational Social Spaces: The Turkish-German Example." In *Migration and Transnational Social Space*, edited by Ludger Pries, 36-72. Aldershot and Brookfield: Ashgate.

Farrington, Anthony, ed. 2004. *Dr Richardson's Missions to Siam 1829-1839.* Bangkok: White Lotus.

Federation of Trade Unions Burma. 2006. "Migrant Schools Closed by Pop Phra District." February 24.

Fisher, Teresa. A., Linda Mattews, Mary E. Stafford, Kathryn Nakagawa, and Katie Durante. 2002. "School Personnel's Perceptions of Effective Programs for Working with Mobile Students and Families." *The Elementary School*

Journal 102(4): 317-333.

Flynn, Donna F. 1997. "'We Are the Border': Identity, Exchange, and the State along the Benin-Nigeria Border." *American Ethnologist* 24(2): 311-330.

Fong, Vanessa L., and Rachel Murphy, eds. 2006. *Chinese Citizenship: Views from the Margins*. Oxford: Routledge.

Frank, Andre Gunder. 1969. *Latin America: Underdevelopment or Revolution*. New York, NY: Monthly Review Press.

Frasch, Tilman. 2002. "Coastal Peripheries during the Pagan Period." In *The Maritime Frontier of Burma: Exploring Political, Cultural and Commercial Interaction in the Indian Ocean World, 1200-1800*, edited by Jos Gommans and Jacques Leider, 59-78. Amsterdam: Koninklijke Nederlandse Akademie van Wetenschappen.

Furnivall, John S. 1944. *Netherlands India: A Study of Plural Economy*. Cambridge: Cambridge University Press.

———. 1956. *Colonial Policy and Practice: A Comparative Study of Burma and Netherlands India*. New York, NY: New York University Press.

———. 1991 [1939]. *The Fashioning of Leviathan: The Beginnings of British Rule in Burma*. Canberra: Department of Anthropology, Australian National University.

Fusfeld, Daniel R., and Timothy Bates. 1984. *The Political Economy of the Urban Ghetto*. Carbondale: Southern Illinois University Press.

Gately, Gary. 2016. "In Thailand, $3 a Month Could Boost Migrant Health." *Global Health Now*.

Gibson, Margaret A. 1985. "Collaborative Educational Ethnography: Problems and Profits." *Anthropology & Education Quarterly* 16(2): 124-148.

Gibson, Margaret A., and John U. Ogbu. 1991. *Minority Status and Schooling: A Comparative Study of Immigrant and Involuntary Minorities*. New York, NY: Garland.

Giddens, Anthony. 1979. *Central Problems in Social Theory: Action, Structure and Contradiction in Social Analysis*. London: Macmillan.

———. 1984. *The Constitution of Society: Outline of the Theory of Structuration*. Cambridge: Polity Press.

Glassman, Jim. 2010. *Bounding the Mekong: The Asian Development Bank, China, and Thailand*. Honolulu, HI: University of Hawai'i Press.

Glinos, Irene A., Rita Baeten, Matthias Helble, and Hans Maarse. 2010. "A Typology of Cross-Border Patient Mobility." *Health & Place* 16(6): 1145-1155.

Gobbo, Francesca. 2009. "Moving Lives: A Reflective Account of a Three

Generation." In *Traveller, Nomadic and Migrant Education*, edited by Patrick Alan Danaher, Máirín Kenny and Judith Remy Leder, 13-28. New York, NY: Routledge.

Gottlieb, Nora, Dani Filc, and Nadav Davidovitch. 2012. "Medical Humanitarianism, Human Rights and Political Advocacy: The Case of the Israeli Open Clinic." *Social Science & Medicine* 74(6): 839-845.

Grave, Peter. 1995. "Beyond the Mandala: Buddhist Landscapes and Upland-Lowland Interaction in North-West Thailand AD 1200−1650." *World Archaeology* 27(2): 243-265.

Guinard, Caroline. 2006. "Promising 'Education for All' in Thailand: What are the True Benefits for Migrant Children Behind This New Policy." *Burma Issues Newsletter* 16(2): 6-7.

Grundy-Warr, Carl. 2004. "The Silence and Violence of Forced Migration: The Myanmar-Thailand Border." In *International Migration in Southeast Asia*, edited by Aris Ananta and Evi Nurvidya Arifin, 228-272. Singapore: Institute of Southeast Asian Studies.

Grundy-Warr, Carl, Ananda Rajah, Elaine Wong Siew Yin, and Zulkifli Ali. 1997. "Power, Territoriality and Cross-Border Insecurity: Regime Security as an Aspect of Burma's Refugee Crisis." *Geopolitics and International Boundaries* 2(2): 70-115.

Grundy-Warr, Carl, and Elaine Wong Siew Yin. 2002. "Geographies of Displacement: The Karenni and the Shan across the Myanmar-Thailand Border." *Singapore Journal of Tropical Geography* 23(1): 93-122.

Gupta, Akhil, and James Ferguson. 1997. "Beyond 'Culture': Space, Identity, and the Politics of Difference." In *Culture, Power, Place: Exploration in Critical Anthropology*, edited by Akhil Gupta and James Ferguson, 33-51. Durham and London: Duke University Press.

Hall, David. 1981. *A History of South-East Asia*. Hampshire and New York: Palgrave Macmillan.

Hallett, Holt S. 1890. *A Thousand Miles on an Elephant in the Shan States*. Edinburgh and London: William Blackwood and Sons.

Halliday, Robert. 1913. "Immigration of the Mons into Siam." *Journal of the Siam Society* 10(3): 1-13.

———. 1917. *The Talaings*. Rangoon: Superintendent, Government Printing, Burma.

Hannerz, Ulf. 1996. *Transnational Connections: Culture, People, Places*. London and New York: Routledge.

Harvey, Godfrey E. 1967. *History of Burma: From the Earliest Times to March 10 1824, the Beginning of the English Conquest*. London: Cass.

Health Information System Working Group. 2015. *The Long Road to Recovery: Ethnic and Community-Based Health Organizations Leading the Way to Better Health in Eastern Burma.* Mae Sot: Health Information System Working Group.

Hien, Duc Do. 1999. *The Vietnamese Americans*. Westport, CT: Greenwood Press.

Hinton, Peter. 2000. "Where Nothing Is as It Seems: Between Southeast China and Mainland Southeast in the 'Post-Socialist' Era." In *Where China Meets Southeast Asia: Social and Cultural Change in the Border Regions*, edited by Grant Evans, Christopher Hutton and Kuah Khun Eng, 7-27. Singapore: Institute of Southeast Asian Studies.

Hirsch, Philip. 1995. "Thailand and the New Geopolitics of Southeast Asia: Resource and Environmental Issues." In *Counting the Costs: Economic Growth and Environmental Change in Thailand*, edited by Jonathan Rigg, 235-259. Singapore: Institute of Southeast Asian Studies.

Holmes, Seth M. 2012. "The Clinical Gaze in the Practice of Migrant Health: Mexican Migrants in the United States." *Social Science & Medicine* 74(6): 873-881.

Horstmann, Alexander. 2011. "Ethical Dilemmas and Identifications of Faith-Based Humanitarian Organizations in the Karen Refugee Crisis." *Journal of Refugee Studies* 24(3): 513-532.

Horstmann, Alexdander, and Reed L. Wadley, eds. 2006. *Centering the Margin: Agency and Narrative in Southeast Asian Borderlands*. New York and Oxford: Berghahn Books.

Horton, Sarah, and Stephanie Cole. 2011. "Medical Returns: Seeking Healthcare in Mexico." *Social Science & Medicine* 72(11): 1846-1852.

Hovemyr, Anders P. 1989. *In Search of the Karen King: A Study in Karen Identity with Special Reference to 19th Century Karen Evangelism in Northern Thailand.* Stockholm: University of Uppsala.

Htin Aung, Maung. 1967. *A History of Burma.* New York, NY: Columbia University Press.

Huffman, Samantha A., Jaap Veen, Monique M. Hennink, and Deborah A. McFarland. 2012. "Exploitation, Vulnerability to Tuberculosis and Access to Treatment among Uzbek Labor Migrants in Kazakhstan." *Social Science & Medicine* 74(6): 864-872.

Human Rights Watch. 2007. "Burma: Army and Its Proxies Threaten Refugee Camps." April 14.

Inkeles, Alex. 1969. "Making Men Modern: On the Causes and Consequences of Individual Change in Six Countries." *American Journal of Sociology* 75(2): 208-225.

International Labour Organization (ILO). 2005. *Human Trafficking and Forced Labour Exploitation: Guidance for Legislation and Law Enforcement*. Geneva: ILO.

———. 2013. *Transitioning from the Informal to the Formal Economy*. Geneva: ILO.

International Organization for Migration (IOM). 2013. "Migrant Information Note." Issue #21.

———. 2016. *Hazard Exposure and Vulnerability of Migrants in Thailand*, Geneva: IOM.

Irrawaddy. 2004. "Thai Customs Seizes Burmese Rice." August 10.

———. 2005a. "Farewell to the Liberated Area." February 25.

———. 2005b. "Burmese Refugees Relocate to Thai Camps." March 30.

———. 2006a. "Thai Senator Reviews Migrant Conditions in Mae Sot." March 20.

———. 2006b. "Thai Authorities Close Migrant Schools in Phop Phra." March 21.

———. 2006c. "New Thai Policy on Migrant Schools Welcomed." May 11.

———. 2006d. "Brain Drain among Exiled Burmese Dissidents." September 7.

———. 2006e. "Urban Burmese Refugees Moved to Border Camps." September 18.

———. 2006f. "Renowned Karen Rebel Leader Dead." December 24.

———. 2006g. "Ten Thousand Attend Gen Bo Mya's Funeral." December 26.

———. 2010. "Ducking and Diving in Mae Sot." May 14.

Ishikawa, Noboru. 2010. *Between Frontiers: Nation and Identity in a Southeast Asian Borderland*. Singapore: NUS Press.

Johnson, Michelle A., and Kristen S. Marchi. 2009. "Segmented Assimilation Theory and Perinatal Health Disparities among Women of Mexican Descent." *Social Science & Medicine* 69(1): 101-109.

Jonsson, Hjorleifur. 2005. *Mien Relations: Mountain People and State Control in Thailand*. Ithaca and London: Cornell University Press.

Karen News. 2012. "Abhisit Promises to Push for Education Funding for Border Groups." December 13.

———. 2013. "Peace Prize Recipient Honoured for Burma Border Clinic: Australia Cuts Her Funding." November 6.

———. 2016. "International Workers Day Raises Concerns about Equality, Rights and Pay for Burmese Workers." May 3.

Kearney, Michael. 1991. "Borders and Boundaries of State and Self at the End of Empire." *Journal of Historical Sociology* 4(1): 52-74.

Keyes, Charles F. 1979. "The Karen in Thai History and the History of the

Karen in Thailand." In *Ethnic Adaptation and Identity: The Karen on the Thai Frontier with Burma*, edited by Charles F. Keyes, 25-61. Philadelphia: Institute for the Study of Human Issues.

Khin Maung Nyunt. 1988. *Market Research of Principal Exports and Imports of Burma with Special Reference to Thailand (1970/71 to 1985/86).* Bangkok: Institute of Asian Studies, Chulalongkorn University.

Kraft, Richard J. 2004. *Thailand/Burma Health and Education Activities Review: Education Sector Final Rep*ort. Washington, DC: USAID and MSI.

Krause, Kristine. 2008. "Transnational Therapy Networks among Ghanaians in London." *Journal of Ethnic and Migration Studies* 34(2): 235-251.

Lamb, Vanessa. 2014. "'Where is the Border?' Villagers, Environmental Consultants and the 'Work' of the Thai-Burma Border." *Political Geography* 40: 1-12.

Lang, Hazel. 2001. "The Repatriation Predicament of Burmese Refugees in Thailand: A Preliminary Analysis." Working Paper No. 46, UNHCR.

———. 2002. *Fear and Sanctuary: Burmese Refugees in Thailand.* Ithaca, NY: Cornell Southeast Asia Program Publications.

Leach, Edmund R. 1964 [1954]. *Political Systems of Highland Burma: A Study of Kachin Social Structure.* Boston, MA: Beacon Press.

Lee, Jane YeonJae, Robin A. Kearns, and Wardlow Friesen. 2010. "Seeking Affective Healthcare: Korean Immigrants' Use of Homeland Medical Services." *Health & Place* 16(1): 108-115.

Lee, Sang Kook. 2001. "The Adaptation and Identities of the Karen Refugees: A Case Study of Mae La Refugee Camp in Northern Thailand." MA Thesis, Seoul National University.

———. 2012. "Scattered but Connected: Karen Refugees' Networking in and beyond the Thailand-Burma Borderland." *Asian and Pacific Migration Journal* 21(2): 263-285.

Lefebvre, Henri. 1991. *The Production of Space.* Oxford: Blackwell.

Lein, Laura. 1975. "You Were Talkin' Though, Oh Yes, You Was: Black American Migrant Children: Their Speech at Home and School." *Council on Anthropology and Education Quarterly* 6(4): 1-11.

Levitt, Peggy. 2001. *The Transnational Villagers.* Berkeley, CA: University of California Press.

Lieberman, Victor B. 1978. "Ethnic Politics in Eighteenth-Century Burma." *Modern Asian Studies* 12(3): 455-482.

———. 1980. "Europeans, Trade, and the Unification of Burma, c. 1540-1620." *Oriens Extremus* 27(2): 203-226.

———. 1984. *Burmese Administrative Cycles: Anarchy and Conquest, c. 1580-1760.* Princeton, NJ: Princeton University Press.

Lin, Shaun, and Carl Grundy-Warr. 2012. "One Bridge, Two Towns and Three Countries: Anticipatory Geopolitics in the Greater Mekong Subregion." *Geopolitics* 17(4): 952-979.

Lintner, Bertil. 1999. *Burma in Revolt: Opium and Insurgency since 1948.* Chiang Mai: Silkworm Books.

Lomnitz, Larissa A. 1988. "Informal Exchange Networks in Formal Systems: A Theoretical Model." *American Anthropologist* 90(1): 42-55.

Loong, Shona. 2019. "The Neoliberal Borderscape: Neoliberalism's Effects on the Social Worlds of Migrants along the Thai-Myanmar Border." *Political Geography* 74: 1-9.

López, Gerardo R., Jay D. Scribner, and Kanya Mahitivanichcha. 2001. "Redefining Parental Involvement: Lessons from High-Performing Migrant-Impacted Schools." *American Educational Research Journal* 38(2): 253-288.

Mae Sot Labour Office. 2005. "Baep Rai Ngan Phonkan Ook Bai Anuyat Thamngan Raeng Ngan Tangdao (Phama Lao Kamphucha), Wan Thi 1 Mithunayon - 17 Mokarakhom" [Report Form Issuance of Work Permits for Foreign Workers (Myanmar, Laos, Cambodia), June 1, 2004 - January 17, 2005].

Mae Tao Clinic (MTC). 1989-2016. *Annual Reports.* Mae Sot: Mae Tao Clinic.

———. 2010. *From Rice Cooker to Autoclave at Dr. Cynthia's Mae Tao Clinic: Twenty Years of Health, Human Rights and Community Development in the Midst of War.* Mae Sot: Mae Tao Clinic.

Macias, Jose. 1996. "Resurgence of Ethnic Nationalism in California and Germany: The Impact on Recent Progress in Education." *Anthropology & Education Quarterly* 27(2): 232-252.

MacLeod, Jay. 1995. *Ain't No Makin' It: Aspirations and Attainment in a Low-Income Neighborhood.* Boulder, CO: Westview Press.

Maneepong, Chuthatip. 2002/2003. "Policy Thinking and Impact of Economic Promotion in Border Towns, Thailand." *Tinjauan: Policy and Management Review* 5: 75-98.

———. 2004. "Comparative Borderland Developments in Thailand." *ASEAN Economic Bulletin* 21(2): 135-166.

———. 2005. "Dynamics of Industrial Development on Border Region of Laos-Myanmar-Thailand." In *The Naga Challenged: Southeast Asia in the Winds of Change*, edited by Victor R. Savage and May Tan-Mullins, 255-298. Singapore: Marshall Cavendish Academic.

———. 2006. "Regional Policy Thinking and Industrial Development in Thai

Border Towns." *Labour and Management in Development Journal* 6(4): 1-29.

———. 2010. *Dynamics of Cross Border Industrial Development in Mekong Sub-Region: A Case Study of Thailand.* KG, Saarbrücken: Lambert Academic Publishing.

Manida Adisaisakol, and Alicia L. Manondog. 2010. *Education for All: Migrant Education in Practice*. Mae Sot: Migrant Educational Co-ordination Center.

MAP Foundation, and Clean Clothes Campaign. 2014. *Migrant Workers in Thailand's Garment Factories*. Chiang Mai and Amsterdam: MAP Foundation and Clean Clothes Campaign.

Marable, Manning. 2015. *How Capitalism Underdeveloped Black America: Problems in Race, Political Economy, and Society*. Chicago, IL: Haymarket Books.

Marcuse, Peter. 1996. "Space and Race in the Post-Fordist City: The Outcast Ghetto and Advanced Homelessness in the United States Today." In *Urban Poverty and the Underclass: A Reader*, edited by Enzo Mingione, 176-216. Oxford: Blackwell.

Marrow, Helen B. 2012. "Deserving to a Point: Unauthorized Immigrants in San Francisco's Universal Access Healthcare Model." *Social Science & Medicine* 74(6): 846-854.

Massey, Doreen. 1991. "A Global Sense of Place." *Marxism Today* 38: 24-29.

Massey, Douglas, and Nancy Denton. 1993. *American Apartheid: Segregation and the Making of the Underclass.* Cambridge, MA: Harvard University Press.

Maung Aung Myoe. 2002. *Neither Friend Nor Foe: Myanmar's Relations with Thailand since 1988: A View from Yangon*. Singapore: Institute of Defence and Strategic Studies, Nanyang Technological University.

McCarthy, James. 1994 [1900]. *Surveying and Exploring in Siam*. Bangkok: White Lotus.

Meier, Benjamin Mason, and William Onzivu. 2014. "The Evolution of Human Rights in World Health Organization Policy and the Future of Human Rights through Global Health Governance." *Public Health* 128(2): 179-187.

Migdal, Joel S. 1988. *Strong Societies and Weak States: State-Society Relations and State Capabilities in the Third World.* Princeton, NJ: Princeton University Press.

———. 1998. "Why Do So Many States Stay Intact?" In *Weak and Strong States in Asia-Pacific Societies*, edited by Peter Dauvergne, 11-37. Canberra: Allen & Unwin.

———. 2001. *State in Society: Studying How States and Societies Transform and Constitute One Another*. Cambridge: Cambridge University Press.

Migrant Educational Co-ordination Center. 2010. *Education for All: Migrant*

Education in Practice, 2008-2010. Mae Sot: Education Service Area 2 of Tak Province.

Minghi, Julian V. 1991. "From Conflict to Harmony in Border Landscapes." In *The Geography of Border Landscapes*, edited by Dennis Rumley and Julian V. Minghi, 15-30. London and New York: Routledge.

Mladovsky, Philipa. 2009. "A Framework for Analysing Migrant Health Policies in Europe." *Health Policy* 93(1): 55-63.

Moldenhawer, Boletter. 2005. "Transnational Migrant Communities and Education Strategies among Pakistani Youngsters in Denmark." *Journal of Ethnic and Migration Studies* 31(1): 51-78.

Mya Than. 1992. *Myanmar's External Trade: An Overview in the Southeast Asian Context*. Singapore: Institute of Southeast Asian Studies.

Myat Thein. 2004. *Economic Development of Myanmar*. Singapore: Institute of Southeast Asian Studies.

Nai Banchaphusmasathan. 1985. "A Thai Government Survey of the Middle Salween, 1890." In *The Burma-Thailand Frontier over Sixteen Decades: Three Descriptive Documents* (Constance Wilson, trans.). Athens, OH: Ohio University Southeast Asia Studies.

Nation. 2004. "Drama in Rangoon: Khin Nyunt Ousted." October 20.

———. 2013. "Pradit Floats Idea for a Regional Health Fund." June 15.

Office of the Education Council of the Ministry of Education. 2008. *Educational Provision for Stateless and Cross National Migrant Children in Thailand.* Bangkok: Office of the Education Council.

Ogbu, John U. 1982. "Cultural Discontinuities and Schooling." *Anthropology and Education Quarterly* 13(4): 290-307.

———. 1989. "The Individual in Collective Adaptation: A Framework for Focusing on Academic Underperformance and Dropping Out among Involuntary Minorities." In *Dropouts from School*, edited by Lois Weis, Eleanor Farrar and Hugh G. Petrie, 181-204. Albany, NY: State University of New York Press.

———. 1991. "Involuntary Minorities." In *Minority Status and Schooling*, edited by Margaret A. Gibson and John U. Ogbu, 3-22. New York, NY: Garland.

Oh, Su-Ann. 2016. "Navigating Learning, Employment and Economies in the Mae Sot-Myawaddy Borderland1." In *Myanmar's Mountain and Maritime Borderscapes: Local Practices, Boundary-Making and Figured Worlds*, edited by Su-Ann Oh, 191-211. Singapore: Institute of Southeast Asian Studies.

Ohmae, Kenichi. 1990. *The Borderless World: Power and Strategy in the Interlinked Economy*. New York, NY: Haper Business.

Orfield, Gary. 1998. "Commentary." In *Crossings: Mexican Immigration in*

Interdisciplinary Perspectives, edited by Marcelo M. Suárez-Orozco, 248-249. Cambridge, MA: Harvard University Press.

Pamaree Surakiat. 2005a. "Thai-Burmese Warfare During the Sixteenth Century and the Growth of the First Toungoo Empire." *Journal of the Siam Society* 93: 69-100.

———. 2005b. "The Changing Nature of Conflict Between Burma and Siam as Studied from the Growth and Development of Burmese States from 16th to 19th Centuries." Paper Presented at the SEASREP 10th Anniversary Conference: Southeast Asia, a Global Crossroads, Chiang Mai, Thailand, December 8-9.

Panitch, Leo. 1996. "Rethinking the Role of the State." In *Globalization: Critical Reflections*, edited by James H. Mittelman, 83-113. Boulder, CO: Lynne Rienner.

Park, Robert. 1926. "The Urban Community as a Spatial Pattern and a Moral Order." In *The Urban Community*, edited by Ernest W. Burgess, 3-18. Chicago: University of Chicago Press.

Parsons, Talcott. 1991 [1951]. *The Social System*. London: Routledge.

Pattana Kitiarsa. 2014. *The "Bare Life" of Thai Migrant Workmen in Singapore*. Chiang Mai: Silkworm Books.

Pavlish, Carol Lynn, Sahra Noor, and Joan Brandt. 2010. "Somali Immigrant Women and the American Healthcare System: Discordant Beliefs, Divergent Expectations, and Silent Worries." *Social Science & Medicine* 71(2): 353-361.

Peach, Ceri. 2003. "The Ghetto and the Ethnic Enclave." In *Migration and Immigrants: Between Policy and Reality, A Volume in Honor of Hans van Amersfoort*, edited by Jeroen Doomernik and Hans Knippenberg, 99-122. Amsterdam: Aksant Academic Publishers.

Pearson, Ruth, and Kyoko Kusakabe. 2012. "Who Cares? Gender, Reproduction, and Care Chains of Burmese Migrant Workers in Thailand." *Feminist Economics* 18(2): 149-175.

Phianphachong Intarat. 2018. "From SEZs to Thailand 4.0: Geopolitics of Borderlands in the Thai State's Vision." *Forest and Society* 2(1): 65-78.

Pitch Pongsawat. 2007. "Border Partial Citizenship, Border Towns, and Thai-Myanmar Cross-Border Development: Case Studies at the Thai Border Towns." PhD Thesis, The University of California, Berkeley.

Portes, Alejandro. 1996a. "Global Villagers: The Rise of Transnational Communities." *American Prospect* 25: 74-77.

———. 1996b. "Transnational Communities: Their Emergence and Significance in the Contemporary World-System." In *Latin America in the World-Economy*, edited by Robert Patricio Korzeniewicz and William C. Smith, 151-168.

Westport, CT: Greenwood Press.

Portes, Alejandro, and William Haller. 2005. "The Informal Economy." In *Handbook of Economic Sociology*, edited by Neil J. Smelser and Richard Swedberg, 403-425. New York, NY: Russell Sage Foundation.

Premjai Vungsiriphisal. 2011. "The Challenge of Education Policy for Migrant Children in Thailand from Security Standpoints." Working Papers on Area Studies No. 107, Center for Southeast Asian Studies, Kyoto University.

Race, Jeffrey. 1974. "The War in Northern Thailand." *Modern Asian Studies* 8(1): 85-112.

Rajah, Ananda. 1990. "Ethnicity, Nationalism and the Nation-State: The Karen in Burma and Thailand." In *Ethnic Groups across National Boundaries in Mainland Southeast Asia*, edited by Gehan Wijeyewardene, 102-133. Singapore: Institute of Southeast Asian Studies.

———. 1994. "Burma: Protracted Social Conflict and Population Movements." Paper Presented at the International Conference on Transnational Migration in the Asia-Pacific Region: Problems and Prospects, Bangkok, Thailand, December 1-2.

Rajaram, Prem Kumar, and Carl Grundy-Warr. 2004. "The Irregular Migrant as Homo Sacer: Migration and Detention in Australia, Malaysia, and Thailand." *International Migration* 42(1): 33-64.

Rau, Jon L., and Clive Hughes. 1985. "Significance of 13th-15th Century Ceramics and Other Artifacts in Upland Burial Sites of the Tak-Mae Sot-Umphang Region, Western Thailand." *The Siam Society's Newsletter* 1(2): 1-21.

Reddy, Malavika. 2017. "Law in Mae Sot, Law and Thailand." PhD Thesis, The University of Chicago.

Reid, Anthony. 1988. *Southeast Asia in the Age of Commerce 1450-1680 Volume One: The Lands below the Winds*. Chiang Mai: Silkworm Books.

———. 1993. *Southeast Asia in the Age of Commerce 1450-1680 Volume Two: Expansion and Crisis*. Chiang Mai: Silkworm Books.

Renard, Ronald. 1980a. "Kariang: History of Karen-Tai Relations from the Beginnings to 1923." PhD Thesis, The University of Hawai'i.

———. 1980b. "The Role of the Karens in Thai Society during the Early Bangkok Period, 1782-1873." *Contributions to Asian Studies* 15: 15-28.

Reuters. 2014. "Thai Junta's Pledge to Send Back Myanmar Refugees Sparks Concern." July 14.

Rex, John. 1980. "The Plural Society in Sociological Theory." In *Sociology of South-East Asia*, edited by Hans-Dieter Evers, 97-103. Kuala Lumpur: Oxford University Press.

Rostow, Walt W. 1960. *The Stages of Economic Growth: A Non-Communist Manifesto*. Cambridge: Cambridge University Press.

Sargent, Carolyn, and Stéphanie Larchanché. 2011. "Transnational Migration and Global Health: The Production and Management of Risk, Illness, and Access to Care." *Annual Review of Anthropology* 40: 345-361.

Save the Children, and World Education. 2015. *Pathways to a Better Future: A Review of Education for Migrant Children in Thailand.* Bangkok: Save the Children and World Education.

Schoenberger, Laura, and Sarah Turner. 2008. "Negotiating Remote Borderland Access: Small-Scale Trade on the Vietnam-China Border." *Development and Change* 39(4): 667-696.

Scott, James C. 2009. *The Art of Not Being Governed: An Anarchist History of Upland Southeast Asia*. New Haven, CT: Yale University Press.

Sennett, Richard. 1994. *Flesh and Stone: The Body and the City in Western Civilization.* New York, NY: W.W. Norton.

Seo, Bo Kyeong. 2016. "Patient Waiting: Care as a Gift and Debt in the Thai Healthcare System." *Journal of Royal Anthropological Institute* 22(2): 279-295.

Sharples, Rachel. 2020. *Spaces of Solidarity: Karen Activism in the Thailand-Burma Borderlands*. New York, NY: Berghahn Books.

Smith, Martin. 1999a. *Burma: Insurgency and the Politics of Ethnicity*. London: Zed Books.

———. 1999b. "Ethnic Conflict and the Challenge of Civil Society in Burma." In *Strengthening Civil Society in Burma: Possibilities and Dilemmas for International NGOs*, edited by Burma Center Netherlands (BCN) and Transnational Institute (TNI), 15-53. Chiang Mai: Silkworm Books.

Smith, Michael P., and Luis Guarnizo, eds. 1998. *Transnationalism from Below.* New Brunswick, NJ: Transaction Publishers.

Sobo, Elisa J. 2009. "Medical Travel: What It Means, Why It Matters." *Medical Anthropology* 28(4): 326-335.

Soguk, Nevzat. 1999. *States and Strangers: Refugees and Displacements of Statecraft*. Minneapolis, MN: University of Minnesota Press.

Spinks, Charles Nelson. 1956. "Siam and the Pottery Trade of Asia." *The Journal of the Siam Society* 44(2): 61-111.

Srisakra Vallibhotama. 1986. "Lua, Lawa and Kaliang: The Highland People's Economic and Political Relationships with Those in Lowland from the 14th to the 16th Century." *Muang Boran Journal* 12(1): 54-66.

Stehle, Maria. 2006. "Narrating the Ghetto, Narrating Europe: From Berlin, Kreuzberg to the Banlieues of Paris." *Westminster Papers in Communication and Culture* 3(3): 48-70.

Suárez-Orozco, Carola, and Marcelo M. Suárez-Orozco. 2001. *Children of Immigration*. Cambridge, MA: Harvard University Press.

Sunait Chutintaranond. 1990. "Cakravartin: The Ideology of Traditional Warfare in Siam and Burma 1548-1605." PhD Thesis, Cornell University.

———. 2002. "Leading Port Cities in the Eastern Martaban Bay in the Context of Autonomous History." In *Recalling Local Pasts: Autonomous History in Southeast Asia*, edited by Sunait Chutintaranond and Chris Baker, 9-24. Chiang Mai: Silkworm Books.

Swe, Thein, and Paul Chambers. 2011. *Cashing in Across the Golden Triangle: Thailand's Northern Border Trade with China, Laos, and Myanmar*. Chiang Mai: Mekong Press.

Tagliacozzo, Eric. 2005. *Secret Trades, Porous Borders: Smuggling and States along a Southeast Asian Frontier, 1865-1915*. New Haven, CT: Yale University Press.

Tambiah, Stanley J. 1976. *World Conqueror and World Renouncer*. Cambridge: Cambridge University Press.

Tannenbaum, Nicola, and E. Paul Durrenberger. 1990. "Hidden Dimensions of the Burmese Way to Socialism." In *Perspectives on the Informal Economy*, edited by M. Estellie Smith, 281-299. Lanham, MD: University Press of America.

Taylor, Robert H. 1987. *The State in Burma*. London: C. Hurst & Company.

Tej Bunnag. 1977. *The Provincial Administration of Siam*. Kuala Lumpur: Oxford University Press.

Terwiel, Barend Jan. 2002. "Burma in Early Thai Sources: An Essay on Models of Perception." In *The Maritime Frontier of Burma: Exploring Political, Cultural and Commercial Interaction in the Indian Ocean World, 1200-1800*, edited by Jos Gommans and Jacques Leider, 9-23. Amsterdam: Koninklijke Nederlandse Akademie van Wetenschappen.

Thai PBS World. 2009. "Second Thai-Myanmar Friendship Bridge Officially Opens." October 30.

Thailand Burma Border Consortium (TBBC). 2005. *Programme Report: July to December 2005*. Bangkok: TBBC.

———. 2008. *Programme Report: January to June 2008*. Bangkok: TBBC.

The Border Consortium (TBC). 2015. *Programme Report: January to June 2015*. Bangkok: TBC.

The Lancet. 2012. "Editorial: Burma: Health and Transition." *The Lancet* 379: 2313.

Thomas, Felicity. 2010. "Transnational Health and Treatment Networks: Meaning,

Value and Place in Health Seeking amongst Southern African Migrants in London." *Health & Place* 16(3): 606-612.

Thongchai Winichakul. 1994. *Siam Mapped: A History of the Geo-body of a Nation*. Honolulu, HI: University of Hawai'i Press.

Thornton, Phil. 2006. *Restless Souls: Rebels, Refugees, Medics and Misfits on the Thai-Burma Border*. Bangkok: Asia Books.

Toyota, Mika. 2003. "Contested Chinese Identities among Ethnic Minorities in the China, Burma and Thai Borderlands." *Ethnic and Racial Studies* 26(2): 301-320.

Turner, Sarah. 2010. "Borderlands and Border Narratives: A Longitudinal Study of Challenges and Opportunities for Local Traders Shaped by the Sino-Vietnamese Border." *Journal of Global History* 5(2): 265-287.

———. 2013. "Under the State's Gaze: Upland Trading-Scapes on the Sino-Vietnamese Border." *Singapore Journal of Tropical Geography* 34(1): 9-24.

Umar, Abdurrahman, and Gidado Tahir. 2009. "The Telesis of Nigerian Nomadic Education." In *Traveller, Nomadic and Migrant Education*, edited by Patrick Alan Danaher and Judith Remy Leder, 102-116. New York, NY: Routledge.

Van Andel, Tinde, and Paul Westers. 2010. "Why Surinamese Migrants in the Netherlands Continue to Use Medicinal Herbs from Their Home Country." *Journal of Ethnopharmacology* 127(3): 694-701.

Van Daele, Henk, and Jan van Poucke. 1984. "Urban Education in Belgium." *European Journal of Education* 19(4): 385-395.

Van Schendel, Willem, and Itty Abraham, eds. 2005. *Illicit Flows and Criminal Things: States, Borders, and the Other Side of Globalization*. Bloomington, IN: Indiana University Press.

Van Schendel, Willem. 2005a. "Spaces of Engagement: How Borderlands, Illegal Flows, and Territorial States Interlock." In *Illicit Flows and Criminal Things: States, Borders, and the Other Side of Globalization*, edited by Willem van Schendel and Itty Abraham, 38-68. Bloomington, IN: Indiana University Press.

———. 2005b. *The Bengal Borderland: Beyond State and Nation in South Asia*. London: Anthem Press.

Vandergeest, Peter, and Nancy Lee Peluso. 1995. "Territorialization and State Power in Thailand." *Theory and Society* 24(3): 385-426.

Viladrich, Anahí. 2012. "Beyond Welfare Reform: Reframing Undocumented Immigrants' Entitlement to Healthcare in the United States, A Critical Review." *Social Science & Medicine* 74(6): 822-829.

Viruell-Fuentes, Edna A., Patricia Y. Miranda, and Sawsan Abdulrahim. 2012. "More than Culture: Structural Racism, Intersectionality Theory, and

Immigrant Health." *Social Science & Medicine* 75(12): 2099-2106.

Wacquant, Loïc. 2011. "A Janus-Faced Institution of Ethnoracial Closure: A Sociological Specification of the Ghetto." In *The Ghetto: Contemporary Global Issues and Controversies*, edited by Ray Hutchison and Bruce D. Haynes, 1-31. Boulder, CO: Westview Press.

Walker, Andrew. 1999. *The Legend of the Golden Boat: Regulation, Trade and Traders in the Borderlands of Laos, Thailand, China, and Burma*. Surrey: Curzon Press.

Wallace, Steven P., Carolyn Mendez-Luck, and Xóchitl Castañeda. 2009. "Heading South: Why Mexican Immigrants in California Seek Health Services in Mexico." *Medical Care* 47(6): 662-669.

Wallerstein, Immanuel. 1979. *The Capitalist World-Economy*. Cambridge: Cambridge University Press.

Ward, David. 1989. *Poverty, Ethnicity, and the American City, 1840-1925: Changing Conceptions of the Slum and the Ghetto*. New York, NY: Cambridge University Press.

Weiler, Kathleen. 1994. "Schooling Migrant Children: California, 1920-1940." *History Workshop* 37(1): 117-142.

Weis, Lois. 1990. *Working Class without Work: High School Students in a De-Industrialized Economy*. New York, NY: Routledge.

Wertheim, Wim F. 1980. "Changing South-East Asian Societies: An Overview." In *Sociology of South-East Asia: Readings on Social Change and Development*, edited by Hans-Dieter Evers, 8-23. Kuala Lumpur: Oxford University Press.

Westin, Charles. 2003. "Young People of Migrant Origin in Sweden." *International Migration Review* 37(4): 987-1000.

Wijeyewardene, Gehan, ed. 1990. *Ethnic Groups across National Boundaries in Mainland Southeast Asia*. Singapore: Institute of Southeast Asian Studies.

Willen, Sarah S. 2012. "Migration, 'Illegality,' and Health: Mapping Embodied Vulnerability and Debating Health-related Deservingness." *Social Science & Medicine* 74(6): 805-811.

Wilson, Thomas M., and Hastings Donnan. 1998. "Nation, State and Identity at International Borders." In *Border Identities: Nation and State at International Frontiers*, edited by Thomas M. Wilson and Hastings Donnan, 1-30. Cambridge: Cambridge University Press.

Wirth, Louis. 1928. *The Ghetto*. Chicago, IL: University of Chicago Press.

Wolff, Hans, Hans Stalder, Manuella Epiney, Angela Walder, Olivier Irion, and Alfredo Morabia. 2005. "Healthcare and Illegality: A Survey of Undocumented Pregnant Immigrants in Geneva." *Social Science & Medicine* 60(9): 2149-2154.

Wolters, Oliver W. 1999. *History, Culture, and Region in Southeast Asian Perspectives*. Singapore: Institute of Southeast Asian Studies.

World Vision. 2004. *Research Report on Migration and Deception of Migrant Workers in Thailand*. Bangkok: World Vision.

Wyatt, David. 1994. "Education and the Modernization of Thai Society." In *Studies in Thai History*, edited by David Wyatt, 219-244. Chiang Mai: Silkworm Books.

———. 2004. *Thailand: A Short History*. Chiang Mai: Silkworm Books.

Yan, Wudan. 2016. "Only One Country Offers Universal Healthcare to All Migrants." NPR March 31.

Index